A REASONABLE GOD

Ordinary Action in a Supernatural World

Arnie Berg

HYTEC Press

A REASONABLE GOD

Ordinary Action in a Supernatural World

Copyright @ 2011 by Arnie Berg

All rights reserved. Except for brief quotations in critical publications or reviews, no part of this book may be reproduced in any manner without prior permission.

areasonablegod@gmail.com

www.hytecpress.com

ISBN 978-0-9868010-0-6

Preface

This book reflects the benefits of many years of absorbing the insights and knowledge of numerous authors of diverse opinions about the interplay of science and faith. I do not pretend to hold any specialized knowledge or wisdom other than what I have gleaned from what others have shared from their experience. My hope is that this book will serve as a springboard for those interested in diving into the broad pool of writings that have been generated over the last decade, giving some direction in terms of special interests to be pursued. In addition to the many books cited in the Reference section, there are numerous helpful and resourceful Internet sites that can be explored, such as the BioLogos forum, the American Scientific Affiliation site, the Faraday Institute for Science and Religion, and the TalkOrigins Archive.

While the target audience for this book is primarily young adults raised in North American Christian homes, it also appeals to many others who are confronted with extreme expressions of worldviews in conflict. The polarizing influences of metaphysical naturalism and fundamental literalism have perverted the conversation between science and faith. To reject the supernatural on the basis of natural laws is to commit a logical fallacy. The message of this book is that a loving Creator God is compatible with our understanding of the natural world. Faith and science are not incompatible, and one need not reject one in order to accept the other.

My gratitude goes to those who have shared parts of this journey with me, particularly those "members in good standing" of the Nuts & Bolts Study Group for their challenging, insightful and encouraging dialog. In particular my heart and mind have been stimulated by the pastoral and thoughtful Rod Alm, the reflective Doug Forsyth, the inquisitive Barb Forsyth, the enthusiastic Wes Letkeman, the compassionate, ecclesiastical and wise Ken Merrett, and the cerebral and passionate Truitt Wiensz. My thanks also to those who took time to invest themselves in various ways in this particular project, including brother Waldo, Marie Speiser, and especially Glen Klassen. Glen's encouragement to eliminate the opacity and his gentle nudging toward an unembellished writing style has resulted in a document that I hope will make sense to more than just the author. Thanks also to Tom Aechtner for his reconstructive suggestions.

Beyond all measure of my ability to adequately acknowledge, however, has been the contribution of my wife Brenda, who while readily admitting her lack of engagement with the subject matter and her amusement with the 'big brain Bible Study group' still offered her unfailing support.

With all this help, one would think that few errors or omissions would remain. I fear that may not be the case, so any remaining shortcomings are my own.

CONTENTS

What a mess! 7

What is Science? 14

The Nature and Practice of Science 18

A Short History of Science and Views of Creation 27
- THE BIG BANG THEORY 27
- THE EVOLUTIONARY STORY 40
- COMING TO TERMS WITH BILLIONS OF YEARS 52
- HISTORY OF CREATION VIEWS 57

Intelligent Design: In the Spotlight 74
- WHAT IS ID? 74
- WHAT ID SAYS IT IS NOT 79
- HOW DID ID GET ITS START? 80
- ID'S ROLE IN EDUCATION AND THE COURTS 86
- WHAT DO ID PROPONENTS SAY ABOUT ID? 87
- WHAT DO UNBELIEVING SKEPTICS SAY ABOUT ID? 96
- WHAT DO THEISTIC SKEPTICS SAY ABOUT ID? 102
- ASSESSMENT 138

Common Descent, Common Design, Common Sense 143
- MORPHOLOGY 148
- PALEONTOLOGY 149
- BIOGEOGRAPHY 155
- EMBRYOLOGY 165
- GENETICS 173
- BIOLOGICAL BAGGAGE 187
- CASE STUDY – TAKING AN AXE TO DARWIN'S TREE OF LIFE 190
- ASSESSING THE EVIDENCE 198

References and Further Reading	220
Glossary	228
Index	234

What a mess!

"Religion professor Bruce Waltke dismissed from evangelical seminary for accepting evolution." Similar headlines rang out April 9, 2010 after highly respected religion scholar Bruce Waltke challenged the North American evangelical church to accept evolution as a viable explanation for the existence of humanity. Technically, Waltke was allowed to resign, which he did in a gracious effort to avoid hurting the church. Waltke becomes only the last in a line of forward thinking theology teachers in conservative seminaries to lose their posts because of their willingness to engage mainstream science and work towards integrating it with their faith.

While seminaries are losing their teachers, churches are losing their young people. Harvard sociologist Robert Putnam reports that people in their twenties and thirties are giving up on church. "Roughly four times more than in any previous generation say they have no religious affiliation."[1] A recent book by Young Earth Creationist Ken Ham decries the disconnect between growing children and their church experience, drawing a direct relationship between those who most regularly attend Sunday School and those who leave the church, reject the Bible as true, and become morally compromised.[2] Although Ken Ham would likely disagree, one reason for this disconnect is the church's failure to engage science seriously, particularly evolutionary science.

Another Young Earth Creationist initiative, Kentucky's $27 million Creation Museum opened in 2007 as an epicenter in a culture

---

[1] Los Angeles Times, "*Walking away from the church*", October 17, 2010.
[2] Ken Ham, *Already Gone*, May, 2010.

war between a fundamentalist worldview and those who recognize that the fundamentalist explanations fall far short of mainstream science. The center serves as a focal point for ridicule of its many messages that contradict conventional science.[3]

Education is often the target of these misdirected actions. The twentieth century saw a long history of court cases in the United States that attempted to answer the question of what is appropriate to teach in a science classroom.[4] Creationists attempted to bias, or in their view balance biases, by affixing disclaimers to science textbooks.[5]

In debates and presentations, creationists, whether Young Earth or Intelligent Design, have used arguments from science that are shown to be false, yet continue to use the same arguments.[6] The Answers in Genesis organization became so sensitized to this issue that they published an article to document the arguments that should no longer be used![7] What a mess!

---

[3] Over 800 scientists in the surrounding area representing the National Center for Science Education signed the following statement: "We, the undersigned scientists at universities and colleges in Kentucky, Ohio, and Indiana, are concerned about scientifically inaccurate materials at the Answers in Genesis museum. Students who accept this material as scientifically valid are unlikely to succeed in science courses at the college level. These students will need remedial instruction in the nature of science, as well as in the specific areas of science misrepresented by Answers in Genesis."

[4] This history is well documented in Edward Larson, *Trial and Error: The American Controversy over Creation and Evolution*, 2003; Edward Humes, *Monkey Girl: Evolution, Education, Religion, and the Battle for America's Soul*, 2007.

[5] The stickers in Atlanta, Georgia in November 2004 read: "This textbook contains material on evolution. Evolution is a theory, not a fact, regarding the origin of living things. This material should be approached with an open mind, studied carefully and critically considered."

[6] See Donald Prothero, *Evolution: What the Fossils Say and Why it Matters*, 2007. Some of these arguments are "Moon dust thickness proves a young moon", "Wooly mammoths were flash frozen during the Flood catastrophe", "Paluxy tracks prove that humans and dinosaurs co-existed", and "The speed of light has decreased over time".

[7] Jonathan Sarfati, *Moving forward—arguments we think creationists shouldn't use*, Creation **24**(2):20–24, 2002.

What constitutes the impetus for this propaganda war, where the loudest voice or the most frequently repeated message is often confused with the truth? Why all these firings of scholars, court initiatives, judicial challenges, creation museums, videos filled with mistruths, and debates with untenable positions? Many of these misdirected activities are the result of wrong conclusions based on misconceptions about the Bible and its inerrancy, the enterprise of science, the limits of science, and God's role in nature.

Some would see the Bible as a scientific text. Was the Bible written as a scientific text? Obviously not. Is it logical then to expect the Bible to be authoritative on scientific issues? No. Does that mean that the Bible has lost all its authority? Obviously not. Requiring the Bible to speak authoritatively in the domains of both science and theology creates a false dichotomy forcing people to choose between mainstream science and the Bible.

Another misconception is that the whole Bible must be read literally. This view of interpretation does an injustice to the biblical authors and fails to respect their cultural context and choice of genre. What a travesty for a whole way of understanding the world to be held hostage by this single unwarranted belief.

Some people have the misconception that there is a scientific conspiracy to eliminate God and religion from our social constructs. These people fail to recognize that a significant number of scientists are able to integrate their mainstream science with a meaningful and purposeful faith relationship. Another misconception is the belief that any action by God in the world must be empirically detectable. Since the logical conclusion to this misconception is that God's action must make a measurable difference, they frantically search for markers that indicate the divide between what nature does by itself and what God does to override nature.

Misdirected actions with regard to science and faith come from wrong conclusions, and wrong conclusions are the result of common misconceptions. Where do all these misconceptions come from? To a large extent, misconceptions are the result of fear and incomplete understandings. The fear that permeates the Christian community is related to the concern that the foundations of their faith are being undermined by the claims of science. This concern often stems from an incomplete understanding of the limits of science, the relationship of science and faith, and what science actually teaches. Difficult as it may be for some, an adequate understanding of today's science is essential to a buoyant theology, because in the words of Galileo "one cannot tune two strings together by listening to only one."[8] For many Christians, failure to complete their understanding means that their misconceptions are simply the result of a fear of the unknown. The knowledge of the world around us must be positioned within the framework of the knowledge provided by God's Spirit.[9]

The process that has led to this situation is largely a North American, twentieth century phenomenon.[10] The failure of the evangelical church in North America to actively and truthfully engage the natural sciences has been well documented by Mark Noll in his

---

[8] Maurice Finocchiaro, *The Galileo Affair: A Documentary History*, 1989, p. 63. The quotation is from a letter to Monsignor Dini in 1615. The whole sentence reads "When sacred texts have to be reconciled with new and uncommon physical doctrines it is necessary to be completely informed about such doctrines, for one cannot tune two strings together by listening to just one."

[9] In Colossians 2:3, Paul says "In Christ lie hidden all the treasures of wisdom and knowledge."

[10] This history is described in Ronald Numbers, *The Creationists: From Scientific Creationists to Intelligent Design*, 1992.

1994 book *The Scandal of the Evangelical Mind*. The publication of *The Language of God: A Scientist Presents Evidence for God* by Francis Collins in 2006 legitimized for many believers the active engagement of evolutionary thought within the Christian experience, while at the same time polarizing those locked in an uncritical mode of thinking.

The rapid pace of technological and scientific discovery and change continues unabated. From the grand sweep of galactic space down to the frantic and uncertain world of subatomic particles, new understandings raise questions that challenge traditional theological views. In these pages, I wish to examine the nature of the scientific enterprise as it relates to a Christian worldview. Personally, I am convinced of the super-naturalistic idea of God, revealed in the person of Jesus Christ, purely spiritual Creator of this world, and personal agent in the cosmos who answers prayers and performs miracles. Within this framework I earnestly seek to understand how God acts in our world beyond my personal subjective experience.

In writing this text, it is important to note that I adhere to the following essential premises:

1. The universe cannot be adequately explained through ontological materialism.

2. Science plays an explanatory role limited to our senses.

3. Science is the most effective human enterprise ever undertaken in understanding nature, and is highly reliable and trustworthy.

In his book, *Chance and Necessity*, Jacques Monod wrote that "objective knowledge" based on the material world is the *only* source of knowledge, and that it would soon displace what he felt was the irrationality of religious belief.

> Cold and austere, proposing no explanation but imposing an ascetic renunciation of all other spiritual fare, this idea [objective knowledge as the *only* source of real truth] could not allay anxiety; it aggravated it instead.[11]

Ironically, Monod falls into the trap of not having any objective way to support his claim of objective knowledge, and hence concludes with this impoverished point of view. The cosmos is more than simply matter in motion, the result of chance and necessity; a purposeful God is the ultimate cause of nature, life, and our destiny. The assumption that we live in a world with a supernatural dimension is taken to be reasonable, not irrational. The physical world is accepted as real and intelligible, not an illusion or distortion of our senses. In order to form an integrative worldview with these assumptions, we need to form an understanding of how ordinary cause and effect is seen to work within the space and time of that world.

Science can be trusted to give us a fairly close approximation to the physical reality we experience, observe and explore as our world. The fact that science and religion sometimes speak to the same areas causes us to believe that there are some areas of overlap, and that science may inform religion, and vice versa. We will explore the implications of that intersection, examine the physical evidence and its historical record, and survey its effect on Western thought and the North American evangelical church in particular.

---

[11] Jacques Monod, *Chance and Necessity*, 1970, p. 158.

As much as possible I have tried to respect the contextual integrity of the referenced authors. Communicating all the nuances of thought and knowledge in a survey such as this is difficult. For a deeper dive into and a fuller exploration of the highlighted information, readers are encouraged to engage the referenced materials themselves. A glossary is provided at the back of the book to assist with understanding of some of the technical terms.

The journey begins with an examination of the nature of science itself: how it relates to nature and naturalism, its limits, and how it affects our view of the world. This leads to a look at some highlights of the history of science and how these events have impacted the way we think of the cosmos. The next section deals with a particular way of thinking about biological complexity that has developed in the Western world called Intelligent Design (ID). In that section, the proponents and opponents of this movement are examined against the backdrop of the history of science in the last few centuries. In this context, the next topic of interest is a particular aspect of science: the theory of common descent in biological evolution. The efficacy of this theory is compared to the idea of common design from the ID perspective.

My hope is that Christian readers will be challenged to think critically about the intersection of faith and science, thereby obeying the first commandment to love the Lord with our entire mind, in addition to our heart, soul and strength. We do not manipulate our faith to accommodate science; rather our scientific knowledge informs how we think about some aspects of our faith. The lessons we can draw from this experience can be generalized to the larger picture of how Christians can form a rational, credible, comprehensive, coherent and Godly worldview that integrates science and faith.

What is Science?

"The art of the soluble"
Peter B. Medawar

What is science? Some, like Peter Medawar, have defined science as "An enterprise dedicated to asking answerable questions". How do we know what to ask, what we know, or even that we know? The study of epistemology addresses the notion of knowledge and how it relates to concepts such as truth, belief, evidence and validation. Before the 17th century, science was considered synonymous with knowledge. The word itself is derived from the Greek *scientia*, meaning knowledge. During the Enlightenment period the word gradually replaced the term "natural philosophy".[12] The word "science" with its empirical emphasis assumed its modern day usage after Francis Bacon defined the scientific method. As practitioners of natural philosophy became more specialized and professional, they came to be called "scientists".

The scientific method identified by Francis Bacon is characterized by theorizing, observing and experimental testing. Keith Ward calls this revolutionary approach to study of the natural world "brilliantly daring".

> The revolutionary insight was to devise measurable and repeatable sets of observable conditions, to construct theoretical models from which consequences could be deductively derived by a formulatable set of general laws, and to devise ways of showing how observable facts confirm or disconfirm the model. Plato theorized; Aristotle observed; but the world waited until Galileo and Newton for

---

[12] Denis Alexander, *Rebuilding the Matrix*, 2001, p.11.

observation and theory to be brought together by the notion of a repeatable, mathematically formulatable set of observations in carefully controlled and quantitatively described situations.[13]

The word "theory" as Ward refers to it can be defined as a well-tested, explanatory framework that has not (yet) been falsified by experimentation. Theories may be revised and improved as new data is discovered, or falsified and replaced if shown to be inadequate. Some theories are so well-supported by facts that it is unlikely that they will be substantially modified by future experimentation – but they remain "only a theory". Examples include the theories of gravitation, relativity, and heliocentricity. No theory can ever be said to provide "proof"; it can only provide convincing evidence for the explanatory framework.

A scientific *law* is not a confirmed theory as some mistakenly think. A law of nature is more related to a fact, and describes precise relationships and actions, often with a mathematical equation. Laws are based on empirical observation and usually result in the calculation of a constant, as in the case of gravitation.

Another term that causes confusion is that of *hypothesis*. A hypothesis is a proposed explanation for an observation that makes testable predictions. This forms a part of the process that supports the development of a theory. A hypothesis may be confirmed and accepted or disproved and rejected. A confirmed hypothesis provides supporting evidence for a theory, but never proof.

---

[13] Keith Ward, *Divine Action: Examining God's Role in an Open and Emergent Universe*, 2007, p. 81.

C. John Collins defines science as "a discipline in which one studies features of the world around us, and tries to describe his observations systematically and critically."[14] This definition reminds us that science is a human activity that focuses on empirical observation, and requires sound reasoning and neutrality in terms of expected conclusions. Some sciences focus on the regularities of nature, described by the laws of nature, and some focus on the processes of cause and effect that produced historical events. The National Science Teachers Association (NSTA) has a longer definition of science that also speaks to the methods of science:

> Science is a method of explaining the natural world. It assumes the universe operates according to regularities and that through systematic investigation we can understand these regularities. The methodology of science emphasizes the logical testing of alternate explanations of natural phenomena against empirical data. Because science is limited to explaining the natural world by means of natural processes, it cannot use supernatural causation in its explanations. Similarly, science is precluded from making statements about supernatural forces, because these are outside its provenance. Science has increased our knowledge because of this insistence on the search for natural causes.[15]

C. John Collins finds this definition deficient on two counts. The first debatable premise is that all descriptions be in terms of *natural causes* only. Even ignoring the possibility of supernatural causation, for example, human reasoning, thoughts and choices are not a purely

---

[14] C. John Collins, *Science & Faith: Friends or Foes?*, 2003, p. 34.
[15] Cited in C. John Collins, *Science & Faith*, 2003, p. 40.

material process, and thus historical events resulting from this process may not be subject to scientific explanation. The other debatable premise Collins identifies is that the NSTA makes a theological claim that supernatural forces are irrelevant to science, contradicting what the NSTA says science may not do. To correct this deficiency the statement would need to be revised to say "that the natural, human, and social sciences take natural causes as far as they can go in describing the world around us."[16]

Evolutionary theory, of which Darwin's core ideas of "descent with modification", natural selection and gradual change are only a part, is a scientific theory that has withstood 150 years of testing. This theory remains intact in spite of attacks on it from anti-evolutionary voices that confuse the theory with a naturalistic philosophy. Modern comparative genomics has provided a wealth of new evidence that strongly supports the basic arguments of Charles Darwin and confirms the evidence from other areas of inquiry such as morphology, geology, paleontology, and physiology.

Many Christians agree with Galileo that, "When one is in possession of this [scientific information] it is a gift from God."[17] They realize the enormous value of scientific knowledge to the human condition and are applying that gift in a God-honoring way in medicine, agriculture and many other areas. This gift comes with ethical, social and environmental responsibilities basic to human well-being.

---

[16] Ibid, p. 41.

[17] Galileo, "Letter to the Grand Duchess Christina", in Maurice A. Finocchiaro, *The Galileo Affair: A Documentary History*, 1989, p. 105.

The Nature and Practice of Science

> All science, even the divine science, is a sublime detective story. Only it is not set to detect why a man is dead; but the darker secret of why he is alive.
>
> **G K Chesterton**

The Shadow of Scientism

The merging of the practice of science with an atheistic ideology of science is referred to as *scientific naturalism*, or more informally, *scientism*. Scientism is based on the idea of objectivity, that is, nothing can be known except that which is known empirically.

Unfortunately the term itself seems to imply that it is a philosophy which is inherent in the scientific enterprise itself, whereas it would be far closer to the truth to say, as Denis Alexander does, that 'scientism' is parasitic upon science but certainly not part of it. "Scientific naturalism, or scientism, refers to the view that only scientific knowledge is reliable and that science can, in principle, explain everything."[18]

Scientism is based on positivism, an epistemological perspective claiming that only what enters our senses and can be positively tested and verified is real knowledge. Enlightenment thinkers such as Pierre-Simon Laplace and Auguste Comte formalized the idea of positivism thus replacing metaphysics in the history of thought. One of the best known advocates of positivism today is Stephen Hawking, although he is known more for his physics than for his philosophy. Many aspects of positivism have fallen out of favor in today's world as positivism

---

[18] Denis Alexander, *Rebuilding the Matrix*, 2001, p. 273.

does not prove that truth cannot be found in ideas, laws and principles beyond what can be observed. However, most atheistic scientists adopt a "methodological positivism" and limit their epistemology to the supposed objectivity of scientism.

Underlying the view of scientism is the belief that there is a unity of science that fully describes one real world. Sociology can be reduced to psychology, psychology to biology, biology to chemistry, chemistry to physics, and the laws of physics ultimately control everything. In the seemingly arrogant words of Ernest Rutherford, "Physics is the only real science. The rest are just stamp collecting." This reductionist position does not represent scientific knowledge; it is in fact radically metaphysical. This narrow view of reality ignores the emergent properties of constituent entities. As a simple example, hydrogen is flammable and oxygen supports combustion; however, when they combine chemically as water, the constituent entity has the emergent property of being able to quench fire.

Committing to a philosophy of scientism is as much a step of faith as committing to a Creator. The secularist is not without beliefs. The late Carl Sagan is well known for his materialist doxology: "The Cosmos is all there is, or ever was, or ever will be."[19] In an apparently simplistic statement, Bertrand Russell said, "Whatever knowledge is attainable, must be attained by scientific methods; and what science cannot discover, mankind cannot know."[20] Russell appears to be overly optimistic about scientific dominion. For example, science may have difficulty accounting for Russell's memory of the past, such as recalling what newspaper article he read a week ago. This is a general

---

[19] Carl Sagan, *Cosmos*, 1980, p. 1.
[20] Bertrand Russell, "Science and Ethics", from *Religion and Science*, 1961.

problem with the historical sciences like geology and archaeology where we cannot literally place ourselves back in time. In his commitment to scientism, Richard Lewontin is famously known for his declaration that "We take the side of science *in spite* of the patent absurdity of some of its constructs, *in spite* of its failure to fulfill many of its extravagant promises of health and life, *in spite* of the tolerance of the scientific community for unsubstantiated just-so stories"[21] (my emphasis). In a quibble with Lewontin's further assertion that "we cannot allow a Divine Foot in the door", David Berlinski, a secular Jew, responds:

> If one is obliged to accept absurdities for fear of a Divine Foot, imagine what prodigies of effort would be required were the rest of the Divine Torso found wedged at the door and with some justifiable irritation demanding to be let in.[22]

Ironically, for all his agnostic belief, Berlinski acknowledges the limitations of science and recognizes that only in the religious dimension can a *coherent* philosophy of knowledge be realized.

> While science has nothing of value to say on the great and aching questions of life, death, love, and meaning, what the religious traditions of mankind *have* said forms a coherent body of thought. The yearnings of the human soul are not in vain. There is a system of belief adequate to the complexity of experience. There is recompense for suffering. A principle beyond selfishness is at work

---

[21] Richard Lewontin, Billions and billions of demons, *The New York Review*, p. 31, 9 January 1997.

[22] David Berlinski, *The Devil's Delusion*, 2009, p.9-10.

in the cosmos. All will be well.[23]

So here we have an agnostic that while withholding judgement on the truthfulness of the religious traditions of mankind, acknowledges that the system of belief is coherent.

Methodological naturalism

For the purpose of carrying out scientific research and investigation, scientists have informally agreed to limit the explanations for secondary causes to those that we normally see in nature. An invisible intellectual fence is built around their work called *methodological naturalism*. This arrangement allows scientists to keep their experience with the natural world separate from their theological beliefs, whether those beliefs are theistic or atheistic. An atheistic belief system is known as *metaphysical naturalism* because it asserts that there is nothing beyond the material realm.

The introduction of the scientific method was based on a presupposition that physical nature was neutral and distinct from the Divine being and could thus be controlled and manipulated. Formal and final causes were recognized as foreign to physics. Physics would henceforth deal only with efficient and material causes. To Christians like Newton, God's role in this dichotomy was as guarantor that nature was a rational and intelligible order, which human reason, created in the image of the Creator, could hope to understand and control.[24]

---

[23] Ibid., p. xvi

[24] Keith Ward, *Divine Action: Examining God's Role in an Emergent and Open Universe*, 2007, p. 82.

Methodological naturalism makes the point that there are multiple levels of explanation of reality, and that science limits itself to natural, secondary cause and effect. Theology limits itself to the supernatural, primary cause. Mixing explanations in these two levels is known as a 'category mistake'. A category mistake refers to absurdities such as the color of a number or the emotion of a vegetable. Science admits of no inherent purpose or design, whereas theology sees purpose and design as integral to its explanations. The language of science and the language of ultimate purpose, according to Denis Alexander, "are complementary domains of human discourse with their own distinctive categories."[25]

John Lennox applies the label 'mechanism' to the physical realm and 'agent' to the supernatural realm to help avoid the category mistake. He uses the example of a Ford car to illustrate the problem of a category mistake.

> It is conceivable that someone from a remote part of the world, who was seeing [a Ford car] for the first time and who knew nothing about modern engineering, might imagine that there is a god (Mr. Ford) inside the engine, making it go. He might further imagine that when the engine ran sweetly it was because Mr. Ford inside the engine liked him, and when it refused to go it was because Mr. Ford did not like him. Of course, if he were subsequently to study engineering and take the engine to pieces, he would discover that there is no Mr. Ford inside it. Neither would it take much intelligence for him to see that he did not need to introduce Mr. Ford as an explanation for its working. His grasp of the impersonal principles of internal combustion would be altogether enough to

---

[25] Denis Alexander, *Rebuilding the Matrix*, 2001, p. 279

explain how the engine works. So far, so good. But if he then decided that his understanding of the principles of how the engine works made it impossible to believe in the existence of a Mr. Ford who designed the engine in the first place, this would be patently false – in philosophical terminology he would be committing a category mistake. Had there never been a Mr. Ford to design the mechanisms, none would exist for him to understand.[26]

When you have a chance to throw open the hood of the car, are you surprised not to find Henry Ford inside, knowing that he is the agency behind the creation of this car? Are you able to disassemble the car to gain an appreciation of how it actually works? Of course. In fact as you do so, your admiration for the designer of the car increases the more you discover (assuming you are not in the process of comparing brands!).

This begs the question as to whether God as a scientific explanation can be a category mistake. For Thomas Aquinas, the fact that God created the universe "ex nihilo" (out of nothing) was a demonstration that the cosmos was created without a scientific cause. God's creation of the universe stands as a rational explanation, if not a scientific one. Christianity asserts that God continues to work within the created order, not just providentially, but through becoming incarnate in Jesus Christ, in Mary's pregnancy without the benefit of a human male, in the miracles of Christ and ultimately in his resurrection. However, inserting God into the chain of cause and effect becomes a contentious issue in connection with the Intelligent Design movement, as we shall see later.

---

[26] John Lennox, *God's Undertaker*, 2009, p. 45.

Although methodological naturalism limits the scope of allowable explanations, some theists have been critical of it for various reasons. Some in the Intelligent Design movement see it as either a slippery slope to metaphysical naturalism, or as an illegitimate attempt to prevent supernatural explanations in science. Stephen Meyer, in an interview with Lee Strobel, claims:

> Darwinists say they're under some sort of epistemological obligation to continue trying, because to invoke design would be to give up on science. Well, I say it's time to redefine science. We should not be looking for only the best naturalistic explanation, but the best explanation, period.[27]

What Meyer is suggesting is a metaphysical inference to explain a physical phenomenon, which is a mixing of categories. You cannot redefine science in that way. Meyer's colleague, William Dembski, has developed a methodology called an "explanatory filter" (described in *The Design Inference*) that claims to eliminate high probability events due to necessity and small probability events due to chance. If the event cannot be attributed to chance or natural law, and is "specified" by matching a recognizable or functional pattern, it is attributable to intelligent design.

Denis Alexander has very little patience for those with a fascination for generating highly improbable numbers and using them as an explanation. He says:

> If we calculate the chances of complex things coming into being by

---

[27] Lee Strobel, *The Case for a Creator*, 2004, p. 243.

random processes then it is very improbable that this will happen. Of course. We all agree on that....All this does is provide the challenging parameters within which scientists have to work....If something is highly improbable, then most likely it didn't happen that way (although it may have done), and it leaves the challenge to researchers in the field to get on with the hard work of finding out how it did happen. Why do creationists and ID folk spend so much time tilting at windmills?[28]

With that being said, one would think that Alexander would be a strong proponent of methodological naturalism, but he indicates that he does not find the term particularly useful. There are good reasons why a scientist would not invoke God as an explanation for observed effects in the course of daily scientific research.

> The unstated implication is that Christians will somehow leave their faith in God behind at the laboratory door, whereas precisely the opposite is the case. I would therefore suggest simply dropping the term 'methodological naturalism' as being misleading in this context. Why not just talk about 'scientific explanation' for things? That does the job just as well and retains neutrality about the personal world-view of the scientist involved in providing the explanations.[29]

Methodological naturalism may be helpful as a reminder that there are different categories to which explanations can apply. Challenging

---

[28] Denis Alexander, *Creation or Evolution*, 2008, p. 334.
[29] Ibid., p. 186.

theists or atheists who make category mistakes is important to ensure the integrity of both domains.

A Short History of Science and Views of Creation

> Nature and nature's laws lay hid in night,
> God said 'Let Newton Be' and all was light.
> **Alexander Pope, epitaph for Isaac Newton**

In order to properly position our consideration of biological evolution in its context of development on planet Earth, we need to step back and highlight some of the discoveries about nature as they occurred over the last few centuries. Central to the current understanding of nature is the concept of a cosmological origin of an expanding universe.

The Big Bang Theory

Historically, physicists and cosmologists, those who study the universe as a whole, had little to do with each other. Cosmologists studied the origins of the universe, while physicists investigated sub-atomic elements like quarks, neutrinos, and positrons. When evidence for a Big Bang event started to accumulate, the cosmologists and physicists began to take an interest in each other's work.

How did the Big Bang theory come about? The ancient Greeks thought that the earth was the center of the universe, surrounded by three perfect spheres that reflected the perfection of the heavens. The moon circled the earth in the innermost sphere, the sun and planets in a further sphere, and the stars in the outermost sphere. This Ptolemaic view persisted until the Renaissance, when Galileo, Copernicus and

Kepler discovered that the best way to explain the orbits of the planets was to place the sun at the center of the solar system. This paradigm shift to a heliocentric solar system did not come about overnight. There was considerable philosophical and theological commitment to the centrality of man and his home, planet earth, as well as to the idea of the perfection of circles and spheres. Kepler wrote "My first mistake was in having assumed that the orbit on which planets move is a circle. This mistake showed itself to be all the more baneful in that it had been supported by the authority of all philosophers, and especially as it was quite acceptable metaphysically."[30]

Isaac Newton, a devout but unorthodox Christian his entire life, struggled with the concept of the scope of the universe. After formulating his laws of gravity, which applied equally well to apples and planets, he realized that astronomical bodies suspended in a *finite* static universe would tend to aggregate to a central point by their mutual gravitational attraction. To keep galactic bodies from colliding with each other, Newton postulated that only a static and *infinite* universe would solve the problem. This conclusion was entirely consistent with his belief in an infinite God.[31] This was the cosmology of Newton's world, and it was based as much on his philosophical beliefs as his empirical observations.

This general belief continued until the early twentieth century when Albert Einstein began to see the inadequacy of gravitational effects and formulated his General Theory of Relativity. This theory argued that space and time are a four-dimensional continuum which he referred to as *spacetime*. For weak gravitational fields and slow speeds

---

[30] Cited in Timothy Ferris, *Coming of Age in the Milky Way*, 1988, p. 78-79.

[31] A rich history of Newton's life can be found in David Berlinski, *Newton's Gift*, 2000.

relative to the speed of light, Newton's universal law of gravitation is a limiting case of Einstein's theory. Gravity corresponds to changes in the curvature properties of spacetime resulting from objects with mass and acceleration. Physicist John Wheeler described these effects as "spacetime tells matter how to move; matter tells spacetime how to curve."[32]

Einstein was committed to the old idea of a static and infinite universe; however his own equations challenged his views by implying an expanding universe. To compensate for this expansion he added an arbitrary term that he called the *cosmological constant*.

In 1919 Arthur Eddington carried out an experiment during a solar eclipse that verified that distant star light actually bends due to the sun's gravity when passing near the sun, empirically confirming Einstein's prediction and the truth of the theory of general relativity. However, it was not until 1930 when Einstein actually observed the evidence for universal expansion with astronomer Edwin Hubble at the Mount Wilson Observatory that he believed. There he conceded, "New observations by Hubble and Humason concerning the redshift of light in distant nebulae make the presumptions appear likely that the general structure of the Universe is not static."[33]

Edwin Hubble was instrumental during the 1930s in collecting and publishing the data that demonstrated the expansion of the universe. By this time it was acknowledged that the earth is a small rocky planet that orbits a medium-sized star in the remote outback of a galaxy called the Milky Way. The Milky Way itself is but one of billions of other galaxies scattered throughout space, each consisting of several billions

---

[32] John Wheeler, *A Journey into Gravity and Spacetime*, 2000, p. xi
[33] Cited in Robert Jastrow, *God and the Astronomers*, 1978, p. 43.

of stars. Hubble found that the light coming from distant galaxies is consistently red-shifted to a lower frequency than is ordinary white light. Think of red shifting as light being de-compressed or stretched. The implication is that the object creating the light is moving away from the observer, and the further the distance to the galaxy, the greater the red shifting, implying greater speed.

How was this expansion to be reconciled with Einstein's theory? Einstein confessed that the cosmological constant that he added to his equations was wrong. He called this the greatest blunder of his career.[34]

So all galaxies are moving away from us at varying speeds. To understand this model, think of raisins within a loaf of rising raisin bread. As the loaf rises, each raisin grows further distant from *every other raisin*. In the same way, each galaxy in effect moves further away from every other galaxy. The galaxies themselves are not hurtling through space; rather the space that contains the galaxies is itself enlarging. From the perspective of an observer on any one galaxy, it appears to the observer that she is at the center of the universe.

If these galaxies can move farther apart, then conceptually this expansion can be reversed through time. Reversing the outward motion of the galactic bodies brings them closer and closer together over time, until a singular compressed point is reached from which all space, time, matter and energy originate, and it is thought that the laws of physics as we know them no longer apply. This point is called a *singularity*. The

---

[34] An extensive biography of Albert Einstein can be found in Abraham Pais, *'Subtle is the Lord'*, 1982.

time this grand rollback would take has been calculated to be about fourteen billion years.

If you have difficulty conceptualizing the idea of the compression of all matter back into a vanishingly small point, keep in mind that Einstein showed that matter and energy are interchangeable according to $E=mc^2$. The infinite energy within the singularity at the beginning seems consistent with the power we attribute to God, the Creator.

Again, this paradigm shift did not come about without opposition. The resistance was again based mostly on philosophical grounds. British astronomer Fred Hoyle argued for a static, infinite universe, and derisively labeled the singularity event "The Big Bang" and the name stuck. Author Timothy Ferris writes that

> Fred Hoyle damned the theory as epistemologically sterile, in that it seemed to place an inviolable, temporal limitation on scientific inquiry: The big bang was a wall of fire, past which science at the time did not know how to probe. Hoyle found it "highly objectionable that the laws of physics should lead us to a situation in which we are forbidden to calculate what happened before a certain moment in time." He poked fun at the theory's creationist overtone.[35]

The evidence that shattered the steady state, infinite universe model came unexpectedly. In 1965 Robert Wilson and Arno Penzias of Bell Laboratories were calibrating their radio telescope by getting a zero reading against what they assumed was empty space. Instead of the expected absence of radiation, they found radiation that was coming

---

[35] Timothy Ferris, *Coming of Age in the Milky Way*, 1988, p. 274.

from beyond the Milky Way and for which there was no known source. After making sure that this strange signal was not coming from bird droppings on the antenna, they came to realize that what they were measuring was a radiation that had no identifiable source, and that it was equally detectable in every direction and at all times.

To understand this, consider what scientists speculate happened at the Big Bang. A fraction of an instant after the creation event, the rapidly expanding universe was filled with very hot radiant energy. Matter existed in the form of plasma made of disassociated quarks and electrons, rapidly expanding, and cooling as it expanded. After about three minutes the temperature had fallen sufficiently for electrons to collect around nuclei to form the first atoms. Hydrogen, the simplest element, was the first to form out of the quark-gluon plasma filling the universe. Helium, the next simplest element, then formed. Scientists have predicted that under the initial conditions, for every three atoms of hydrogen there should have been one atom of helium. Analysis of matter in space shows that this is in fact the case. After a billion years of expanding and cooling, the clouds of gas formed knots of condensed matter which became embryo galaxies, and within the galaxies stars formed, and around some stars, planets.

A universe beginning with a Big Bang event would have generated extreme heat and light at first that has now dissipated over time throughout the universe as space has expanded. Scientists have used this premise to predict the present temperature of space, and this is referred to as the *cosmic microwave background radiation.*

In 1927, Georges Lamaitre and George Gamow had hypothesized that if the Big Bang theory were to be correct, this dissipating heat, like heat from an opened oven escaping into the surrounding air, might be detected and measured. In 1948 two associates of Gamow, Ralph Alpher and Robert Herman, calculated that this radiation should be expected at a temperature of about 5 degrees Kelvin, just 5 degrees above absolute zero. Without initially realizing it, Wilson and Penzias confirmed this prediction, further confirming the implications of an expanding universe. Later refinements to the predicted temperature brought it to 2.7 degrees Kelvin.

When actually measured by COBE, the Cosmic Background Explorer satellite in 1992, the temperature came within a fraction of a degree of the theorized temperature, providing accurate confirmation of the expansion-time measurement of the universe.

Scientists also knew that there would have to be some irregularities or ripples in the background radiation to account for galaxy formation. Some 'lumpiness' of matter is required for gravity to draw this matter together. The COBE experiment confirmed the existence of these irregularities in space as well.

Philosophical Responses to the Big Bang Event

As fascinating as the Big Bang discovery process has been, equally fascinating are the philosophical implications that many scientists have seen in the observations themselves. In some cases, erroneous conclusions were drawn as a result of mixing categories, and in other cases the conclusions were simply the author's personal view and not intended as an explanation at the scientific level.

Sir Frederick Hoyle said, "The big bang theory requires a recent origin of the universe that openly invites the concept of creation."[36] Hoyle was committed to a static, eternal universe and what he was

---

[36] Fred Hoyle, *The Intelligent Universe*, 1983, p. 237.

implying by 'recent' was that a universe with a beginning somewhat parallels that assertion in the Genesis account from the Bible. Even as late as 1975 Hoyle was insisting that the red shift indicated that the mass of hydrogen was less during earlier times than today[37], and that the cosmic microwave background radiation resulted from a blurring effect of radiation coming from an event *prior to* the time we measure as the beginning of the universe. By this time he had accepted the implications of Einstein's theory, but his reaction was "The universe is supposed to have begun at this particular time. From where? The usual answer, surely an unsatisfactory one, is: from nothing!"[38]

Robert Jastrow, an agnostic, said, "The essential element in the astronomical and biblical accounts of Genesis is the same: the chain of events leading to man commenced suddenly and sharply, at a finite moment in time, in a flash of light and energy...the Hubble Law is one of the great discoveries in science: it is one of the main supports of the scientific story of Genesis."[39] In spite of his questionable assumption that Genesis contains a scientific story, Jastrow ends his book, *God and the Astronomers*, by saying,

> For the scientist who has lived by his faith in the power of reason, the story ends like a bad dream. He has scaled the mountains of ignorance; he is about to conquer the highest peak; as he pulls himself over the final rock, he is greeted by a band of theologians who have been sitting there for centuries.[40]

---

[37] Fred Hoyle, *Highlights in Astronomy*, 1975, p. 164.
[38] Fred Hoyle, *Astronomy Today*, 1975, p. 165.
[39] Robert Jastrow, *God and the Astronomers*, second edition, 1992, p. 14.
[40] Robert Jastrow, *God and the Astronomers*, 1978, p. 105-106

George Smoot, speaking as an astrophysicist and not a theologian, said, "The question of 'the beginning' is as inescapable for cosmologists as it is for theologians...there is no doubt that a parallel exists between the big bang as an event and the Christian notion of creation from nothing."[41]

Arno Penzias and Robert Wilson won the Nobel Prize for Physics in 1978 for their discovery of the CMB radiation of the "Big Bang". Arno Penzias said, "The easiest way to fit the observations with the least number of parameters was one in which the universe was created out of nothing, in an instant, and continues to expand."[42]

His colleague, Robert Wilson also recognized the same implications. "Certainly, if you are religious, I can't think of a better theory of the origin of the universe to match with Genesis."[43]

These are perhaps somewhat naïve theological statements coming from scientists, but they do recognize certain metaphysical implications in their discoveries. With these endorsements for a science-authorized creation story that aligns with the traditional Christian belief in a creation out of nothing, why do unbelieving scientists familiar with the evidence not also readily adopt the Biblical story of redemption? Certainly there have been some, such as astronomer Allan Sandage who became a believer in the God of the Bible at the age of 60. More frequently, however, naturalistic presuppositions result in alternative speculative explanations, such as the oscillating universe, multiverses and quantum fluctuations.

---

[41] George Smoot and Keay Davidson, *Wrinkles in Time*, 1993, p. 189.
[42] Arno Penzias, interview with Fred Heeren, *Show Me God*, 1998, p. 156.
[43] Robert Wilson, interview with Fred Heeren, *Show Me God*, 1998, p. 157.

Leonard Susskind, one of the originators of string theory, is an example of someone with this kind of materialistic thinking. In his recent book, *The Cosmic Landscape*, he describes how quantum fluctuations and the resulting cosmic inflation continuously creates innumerable new universes, each with its own set of physical laws and constants. Thus we should not be surprised that some of these universes have laws which permit life to arise, leading to human life capable of measuring these laws and constants and perceiving them to be extremely fine-tuned for our existence. Out of a collection of all these possible universes, we must find ourselves in a universe that is more fit than the others to support our existence.

However, without scientific evidence that quantum fluctuations can lead to a Big Bang, or that multiple universes are even possible, saying that 'Quantum fluctuations did it' is equivalent to saying 'God did it', clearly an inference to the metaphysical realm. Our observations are limited empirically to *our* universe, so all of these alternative explanations remain speculative attempts to find a naturalistic explanation for a cosmic dilemma. Even if a naturalistic explanation for creation out of nothing were to be substantiated, this would merely answer the question of 'how' God created. The question of 'why' God created requires explanation at a different level.

The Anthropic Principle

Over the years, scientists have reported on many cosmic coincidences that make it possible for intelligent life to exist.[44] Some scientists see

---

[44] One example is Paul Davies, *Cosmic Jackpot: Why Our Universe Is Just Right for Life*, 2007.

this fine-tuning as an example of the Anthropic Principle[45], the result of living in one environment out of many possible environments. The environment wherein we exist is the one where the conditions making it possible for us to observe our environment and its apparent coincidences, are the same as those making it possible for us to exist in that environment. To others the fine-tuning also suggests evidence of design by a super-intelligence. For the Christian, that super-intelligence is God. However, it is a matter of faith, because the evidence for the extreme fine-tuning we observe carries the weight of persuasion; it does not and cannot carry the weight of proof. God has created the world in such a way that the evidence for his existence is compelling for those who are open to it. However, that same evidence is not overwhelming or overpowering enough so as to negate faith. Blaise Pascal was right in saying that God has given evidence sufficiently clear for those with an open heart, but sufficiently vague so as not to compel those whose hearts are closed. For example, for Christians who find the evidence for evolutionary creation compelling, David Wilcox claims that it is not hard to see God's guiding hand at work, but the evidence, while pointing to God, does not prove God's existence.[46]

Faith is always a prerequisite for satisfying God's requirement for a relationship with him. Without faith it is impossible to please him. God has balanced the scale so finely that it takes faith or non-faith to tip it. He has ensured that we submit to him of our own free will, not because we are bowled over by undeniable proof of His existence.

---

[45] There are several flavors of the Anthropic Principle, most commonly mentioned are the Strong and the Weak. Our focus here is on the weak version, which states *"conditions that are observed in the universe must allow the observer to* exist."

[46] David Wilcox, *God and Evolution*, 2004, p.117.

To further clarify the distinction between fine-tuning and what we have referred to as the Anthropic Principle, we turn to Richard Dawkins. Although he is wrong in his conclusion that God and the Anthropic Principle are alternatives, he correctly identifies the nature of the Anthropic Principle when he writes:

> It is a strange fact that religious apologists love the Anthropic Principle. For some reason that makes no sense at all, they think it supports their case. Precisely the opposite is true. The Anthropic Principle, like natural selection, is an alternative to the design hypothesis. It provides a rational, design-free explanation for the fact that we find ourselves in a situation propitious to our existence. I think the confusion arises in the religious mind because the Anthropic Principle is only ever mentioned in the context of the problem that it solves, namely the fact that we live in a life-friendly place. What the religious mind then fails to grasp is that two candidate solutions are offered to the problem. God is one. The Anthropic Principle is the other. They are alternatives.[47]

Dawkins makes the faulty assumption that there *are* alternatives for the Anthropic Principle from which to choose. Although this statement illustrates Dawkins' black and white kind of thinking, he does make the point that fine-tuning and the Anthropic Principle are two different things. Fine-tuning admits no alternatives from which to choose. Our ignorance about alternatives, either of multi-universes or multiple life-friendly planets in the universe, makes it difficult to decide which principle applies. Dawkins also makes a category mistake by

---

[47] Richard Dawkins, *The God Delusion*, 2006, p.136

positioning God and the Anthropic Principle as alternative explanations. To illustrate, we can ask the questions, "Is theism consistent with fine-tuning?", and "Is theism consistent with the Anthropic Principle?" As Berlinski concluded, in both cases we can respond that our existence is not improbable under theism. Now if we ask the questions, "Is atheism consistent with fine-tuning?", and "Is atheism consistent with the Anthropic Principle?", we would answer negatively for the former, and affirmatively with the latter. Again, our ignorance about alternatives makes these questions unfruitful, but it does show that Dawkins is operating under false assumptions.

The Big Bang event has been generally accepted by the scientific community, not because of speculative conjectures about the nature of the universe, but as the result of many converging lines of evidence that support this hypothesis. Strong scientific evidence and quantifiable measurements confirm the Big Bang origin of the universe and an age of the universe that can be measured in billions of years. The experiments that confirm this have been repeated many times over the years, making the Big Bang a well-accepted theory. The main lines of evidence contributing to this conclusion are the following:

1. The General Theory of Relativity implies the expansion of the universe – Einstein

2. Redshift of galaxies implies expansion – Hubble, Eddington

3. Cosmic microwave background radiation – Penzias, Wilson

4. Chronological: Velocity of expansion implies a universe 13.7 billion years old, consistent with the measured age of the oldest stars in the order of 12 billion years old.

5. The red shift of galaxies furthest from us is greater than that of nearer galaxies, implying that the further galaxies are separating from us at a greater rate than nearer galaxies.

The Evolutionary Story

According to biologists, the evolution of life on earth has experienced its own Big Bang, but with a very long fuse because it came not at the beginning of the process, but near the end. This event, known as the Cambrian explosion, was preceded by a long period of time in which life evolved in forms that did not fossilize well. The Cambrian was a time of great evolutionary innovation. One innovation was the development of hard body parts, resulting in better fossilization and preservation of a life history that we can observe today.

How do we define life? Life is the carbon-based organic matter that extracts, transforms, and consumes energy derived primarily either directly or indirectly from the sun and has the property of reproducing itself. Life has the property of sensing and responding to alterations in its environment, and changing gradually and fundamentally over time.

All known life has the same type of complex chemical, molecular organization, based on nucleic acids, carbohydrates, lipids, amino acids and protein. The basic unit of life is the cell, which is structurally composed of diverse molecules. Nucleic acids serve as a central storage and processing control of the genetic code that regulates development and metabolism of the organism. The defined functions for each of an organism's components and the regulated interactions among them are determined largely by their structure and surroundings.[48]

There is some debate about whether or not viruses constitute a form of life since they need to form a symbiotic relationship with a living cell in order to replicate. The definition of life itself resists consensus in unequivocal terms for both scientists and philosophers. There is no debate however about the fact that the elements that combine to form organic metabolites and molecules are the same chemical elements that form inorganic compounds.

How old is the earth? The process of evolution on the host planet Earth as we know it today requires an unimaginable duration of time. The age of the earth is most easily determined by measuring the amount of radioactive decay using the known half-lives of radioactive substances in rocks. Think about how you can fold a piece of paper in half. You can continue to fold the paper in half about six or seven times until it becomes so condensed that folding is no longer possible. Radioactive chemicals also undergo a kind of folding, where half of the matter of the chemical disappears in the form of radioactive energy and subatomic particles over a certain period of time. In most decay reactions that are relevant to the age of the earth, this period of time is measured in millions of years.

Certain nuclides are radioactive isotopes of elements found in nature at detectable levels. The following table (Figure 1) shows a list of all known radioactive nuclides with half-lives of 1 million years or more. Only 23 of the 34 nuclides listed in the table are found in detectable amounts in nature. 'Yes-P' in the table indicates that a

---

[48] David Nelson, Michael Cox, *Lehninger Principles of Biochemistry*, 2008, p. 1-2.

nuclide is present in detectable amounts, but that it is continuously produced as the product of another decay series.[49]

Nuclide	Half-life (years)	Found in nature?	Nuclide	Half-life (years)	Found in nature?
^{50}V	6.0×10^{15}	Yes	^{244}Pu	8.2×10^{7}	Yes
^{144}Nd	2.4×10^{15}	Yes	^{146}Sm	7.0×10^{7}	No
^{174}Hf	2.0×10^{15}	Yes	^{205}Pb	3.0×10^{7}	No
^{192}Pt	1.0×10^{15}	Yes	^{236}U	2.39×10^{7}	Yes-P
^{115}In	6.0×10^{14}	Yes	^{129}I	1.7×10^{7}	Yes-P
^{152}Gd	1.1×10^{14}	Yes	^{247}Cm	1.6×10^{7}	No
^{123}Te	1.2×10^{13}	Yes	^{182}Hf	9×10^{6}	No
^{190}Pt	6.9×10^{11}	Yes	^{107}Pd	7×10^{6}	No
^{138}La	1.12×10^{11}	Yes	^{53}Mn	3.7×10^{6}	Yes-P
^{137}Sm	1.05×10^{11}	Yes	^{135}Cs	3.0×10^{6}	No
^{87}Rb	4.88×10^{11}	Yes	^{97}Tc	2.6×10^{6}	No
^{187}Re	4.3×10^{10}	Yes	^{237}Np	2.14×10^{6}	Yes-P
^{176}Lu	3.5×10^{10}	Yes	^{150}Gd	2.1×10^{6}	No
^{232}Th	1.4×10^{10}	Yes	^{10}Be	1.6×10^{6}	Yes-P
^{238}U	4.47×10^{9}	Yes	^{93}Zr	1.5×10^{6}	No
^{40}K	1.25×10^{9}	Yes	^{98}Tc	1.5×10^{6}	No
^{235}U	7.04×10^{8}	Yes	^{153}Dy	1.0×10^{6}	No

Figure 1. Table of radioactive nuclides taken from Kenneth Miller, *Finding Darwin's God*, 1999

This list falls naturally into two halves at the point where the answer to 'Found in nature?' changes from 'Yes' to 'No'. The short-lived nuclides that have a half-life of 7.0×10^7 years or less are not naturally found on earth. Of the short-lived nuclides that are found in nature,

---

[49] A useful resource for background information is G. Brent Dalrymple, *The Age of the Earth*, 1991. The table is from page 377.

there are known processes in nature that create these nuclides. There is plenty of beryllium-10 (10Be) around, because it is produced by cosmic ray bombardment of dust particles in the upper atmosphere that become incorporated in rainfall and sediment. Manganese (53Mn) is produced in exactly the same way. The significance of these nuclides is that although they are detectable in nature, they are the only nuclides that are produced by natural processes. We assume all other nuclides have been present since the formation of the earth.

Every nuclide with a half-life of less than 80 million years is missing from our region of the solar system, and all the rest are still present. Why? The obvious explanation is that the solar system is much older than 80 million years, and the short-lived nuclides have simply decayed themselves out of existence.

After 20 half-lives, only .0001 percent of a nuclide can still be found. Twenty half-lives of 80 million equals approximately 1.6 billion years, which is long enough to eliminate all the short-lived nuclides. Based on this and other tests, scientists conclude that the best estimate for the age of the oldest rocks on earth is 4.5 billion years. This age is confirmed when the same tests are applied to meteorites. This does not "prove" the age of the earth, but it does result in a list that is exactly what we would expect if the earth is old, and only creates puzzlement if the earth is actually young.

Analysis of tree rings of fossilized bristlecone pines in the Sierra Nevada Mountains shows that the oldest trees date back to 12,000 years. Varve lakes in Japan and Siberia contain alternating layers of seasonal pollen sedimentation that evidently took over 40,000 years to accumulate. Ice layers in Greenland and the Antarctic show accumulations of hundreds of thousands of years. At the current rate of growth, some coral reefs have been growing for over 140,000 years.[50] These are just a few examples showing what clearly appears to be a very old earth.

How did life on earth originate? This is a mystery, but based on the evidence, it seems that life appeared very early after earth was formed about four and a half billion years ago. At first, single celled organisms must have formed from prebiotic organic molecules. There are some people like biologist Stuart Kaufmann who believe that chemical matter has self-organizing properties, and that in the right environment it is capable of transforming inanimate matter into living matter. Alexander Oparin, one of the first to claim that there is no fundamental physical difference between a living organism and lifeless matter, researched the origin of life by focusing on multimolecular systems called probionts interacting with their surrounding solution to become self-replicating.[51] Stanley Miller famously carried Oparin's thesis to the experimental stage in 1953. By simulating what was thought to be early earth's reducing atmosphere of methane, ammonia, hydrogen and water, he was able to artificially synthesize most of the twenty amino acids used to build proteins. However it happened, with life's ability to reproduce, natural selection and adaptation took over to produce ever more complex life forms.

Some of the earliest life forms resemble filamentous blue-green bacteria growing in microbial mats. These mats have fossilized into distinctive rock formations called stromatolites built up of calcium carbonate. Blue green bacteria, like all other single-celled prokaryotes,

---

[50] Darrel Falk, *Coming to Peace with Science: Bridging the Worlds Between Faith and Biology*, 2004, p. 73-74.

[51] Alexander Oparin, *A hypothetic scheme for evolution of probionts*, Origin of Life **5** (1974), p. 223-226.

have DNA, but it is not found in a membrane-enclosed nucleus. This first stage of the evolutionary story lasted some two billion years.

The second stage of the evolution of life is represented by the development of eukaryotic cells from the single-celled organisms of the first stage. Eukaryotic cells have DNA enveloped in membranes and contain the organelles or components we recognize today such as mitochondria and chloroplasts. As these single-celled eukaryotes formed into colonies of cells, different cells of the organism began to specialize and organize into tissues and organs, giving rise to truly multi-cellular organisms. This stage lasted until about 540 million years ago.

The beginning of the third stage was marked by the biological big bang, known as the Cambrian explosion. The first fossilized record of recognizable ocean-based animals appears in great abundance. The Burgess Shale, a rock formation near Field, British Columbia, has yielded large numbers of samples of this era and has a fascinating history documented by Stephen Jay Gould in his book *'Wonderful Life'*. Every body plan that exists today can be traced back to the body plans identified in the Cambrian explosion. *There were even some bizarre body plans in the Burgess Shale that do not exist today; they were evolutionary dead ends.* Surprisingly, the Darwinian model of the tree of life, described as having a few species in the "trunk of the tree" evolving into many "branches", has been inverted into a progression where many body plans, or phyla, are reduced to the narrower classification of body plans that we see today.

Before describing the next stages, we need to understand the mechanism by which evolution works. Evolution works on a trial and error method to arrive at a life form that is more successful than others of the same species within a given environment. There are two principles at work. The first is that mutations happen. The DNA in each cell that controls growth and development is subject to occasional structural genetic changes resulting from 1) chemical accidents, 2) radiation damage or 3) replicating errors. 'Errors' implies that most mutations are damaging, but every now and then a mutation occurs which improves the ability of the life form, or its progeny, to survive better within the environment in which it exists.

The second principle is that there is competition at work. Life forms prosper when their genes are better suited to their environment, and when they live long enough to reproduce. Life forms with inferior genes meet their fate before having a chance to reproduce, or reproduce inferior life forms that eventually come to a dead end. Thus, random mutations together with non-random selection results in life forms continuously evolving into forms better able to survive and reproduce within their environment.

In many ways, natural selection is similar to artificial breeding. The main difference is that in artificial selection a human agent makes the choices as to which animals get to reproduce, whereas in natural selection the environment implicitly makes that choice. For artificial selection the time-frame is very short, but because of the intentional selection of the breeder for desired features, observed change in each generation is accelerated. Artificial selection is obviously much faster in getting results than natural selection because there is much less trial and error from generation to generation.

The phyla of the third stage evolved into all the forms of sea life dominated by fish in the final stage. It is tempting to think that adaptations through natural selection such as strong fins and the development of lungs allowed certain fish to spend increasing amounts of time outside of the water, eventually making land their primary residence as amphibians and eventually reptiles. However, it is also possible that the ancestors of the reptiles were more like wood lice or centipedes that flourished equally well in water and on land, and adapted to land life. Some reptiles evolved into dinosaurs that dominated the ecosphere until about 65 million years ago when they became extinct. Other reptiles evolved into warm-blooded life forms that became mammals. Mammals did not thrive until the dinosaurs disappeared. In the later stages of evolution, from four million years to 100,000 years ago, ape-like hominids appeared that gave rise to modern humans.

That is a very simplistic account of the evolutionary story that provides the best explanation of the fossil record and of the recent discoveries in genetics.

How did this particular explanation come about? Charles Darwin had a lot to do with it. But if it had not been Charles Darwin, there would likely have been someone else in the years following 1859, the year in which the *Origin of Species* was published. Evolution as a scientific hypothesis had been considered for many years prior to Darwin's publication. What Darwin accomplished was to identify the *mechanism* of evolution.

The ideas published in 1859 had percolated in Darwin's mind ever since the completion of his five-year expedition in the good ship Beagle around South America and the Galapagos islands completed in 1836. Alfred Russel Wallace was about to publish essentially the same theory, which prompted the procrastinating Darwin to publish the *Origin of Species* in 1859.

Prior to Darwin, the Newtonian system seemed to suggest the world was a self-sustaining, deterministic mechanism. The industrial revolution encouraged the view of the universe as a machine. The precise order and lawful compliance of nature was seen as reflective of the nature of God. Historian of science and British philosopher Alfred North Whitehead described this expectation of orderly predictability when he said, "There can be no living science unless there is a widespread instinctive conviction in the existence of an *Order of Things*. And, in particular, of an *Order of Nature*." He then went on to argue that the assurance of this conviction lay in the "medieval insistence upon the rationality of God."[52] The "trickle-down theory" which held that the rationality of human thought originated from the rationality of God, was expressed by astronomer Johannes Kepler as "thinking God's thoughts after him."

By the beginning of the 1800s, theologian William Paley had no difficulty applying the same principle to biology. He described a 'natural theology' that suggested that the contrivance of the eye, for example, implied a designer capable of designing and fabricating this complexity, thus suggesting a perfect and beneficent Creator. Although Darwin was strongly influenced by Paley, Darwin was nonetheless troubled by the fact that not all the design in nature demonstrates this beneficence. Quite the opposite: the character of much of nature was 'red in tooth and claw' as described by Alfred, Lord Tennyson.

Within thirty years of Darwin's most important publication, his views were largely accepted. Even many of the leading clergy of the time readily accepted Darwin's thesis. Two significant gaps weakened Darwin's thesis – the incomplete fossil record that showed the

---

[52]Alfred North Whitehead, *Science and the Modern World*, 1925, p. 2-4, 13.

transition from one form of life to another and the lack of understanding of a hereditary mechanism that would preserve beneficial mutations. Darwin expressed confidence that these gaps would be bridged, and over the past 150 years for the most part they have been.

The steady progress in paleontology has unearthed a fossil record that now shows many examples of transitional body forms.[53]

Gregor Mendel, an Austrian monk, initially discovered the hereditary secret. Mendel, a contemporary of Darwin, systematically documented the careful breeding of thousands of pea plants and established the hereditary principles of inheritance. Darwin failed to recognize the significance of Mendel's research, and it was not until the early 20th century that the importance of Mendel's work was realized. This new understanding of genetics formed the basis of the Modern Synthesis in evolutionary biology.

In 1926 Thomas Hunt Morgan exploited the short life cycle of the fruit fly to identify chromosomes as the entities responsible for the transmission of inheritable characteristics. Research into the composition and function of chromosomes and their genes intensified in the next twenty five years until in 1953 Francis Crick and James Watson solved the mystery of the structure of DNA's double helix and thus heredity was understood at the molecular level.[54]

The discovery of genes as the carriers of hereditary information and the understanding of how these genes behaved within populations of species closed the gaps that had troubled original Darwinian thinking

---

[53] See the section on Common Descent for further details.

[54] Interesting accounts of this process can be found in James Watson, *The Double Helix, 1980*, and Horace Freeland Judson, *The Eighth Day of Creation: The Makers of the Revolution in Biology*, 1979

and made the "neo-Darwinian" synthesis possible. The last eighty years of research in this area has done much to answer questions of "nature versus nurture", the nature of disease, and the genetic distance between species. A high point of this research was the completion of the mapping and sequencing of the human genome in 2003. Francis Collins, a well-known American geneticist and highly respected Christian headed the project, succeeding James Watson as head of the National Center for Human Genome Research in 1993.

As early as 2001, the mapping and sequencing of the human genome compared with the chimpanzee genome showed that in the regions that code for proteins and developmental switches the human and the chimpanzee sequences are extremely similar, with a 98% overlap. Additionally humans share large amounts of non-coding areas of the DNA with chimps. What this implies is that even areas that are called 'junk DNA' have been faithfully copied for millions of years. In spite of the fidelity of copying, mutations accumulate in the DNA, and by examining the pattern of mutations in all living entities we can derive a theoretical tree showing the relatedness of one species to another and their common ancestry. This raises some interesting questions. What is it that makes us so different from all other life forms? In view of the genomic similarity to chimpanzees, what mechanisms can explain the uniqueness of humans and the fact that the *Homo sapiens* is alone in the capacity for self-reflection and appreciation of the fact of its own existence? Or, in the words of Granville Sewell,

> When you ask [the modern scientist] how a mechanical process such as natural selection could cause human consciousness to arise out of inanimate matter, he doesn't understand what the problem is, and he

talks about human evolution as if he were an outside observer, and never seems to wonder how he got inside one of the animals he is studying.[55]

Synthesis

If the universe is billions of years old, of what significance is that to our life today? It turns out that life is not possible without the slow development of the universe over billions of years. The only elements created by the Big Bang event itself were hydrogen and helium, and traces of lithium, deuterium and beryllium. All other more complex elements in the periodic table up to iron required the formation of stars and the extreme energy of nuclear fusion. This star forming process required billions of years. Some complex elements such as gold are only formed when a star explodes in a supernova, sending pieces of itself blasting through space to form new stars. Several generations of stars are needed to produce the carbon, nitrogen, sulphur, phosphorous and other essential chemicals of which life consists.

Scientists who have widely differing worldviews may still agree perfectly on the details of this astrophysical process, or that of genetics or evolutionary biology. A worldview, according to Christian scholar Alister McGrath, is a comprehensive way of viewing reality that tries to make sense of its various elements within a single, overarching way of looking at things. Some people like Francis Collins embrace the Christian faith without reservation. Others like James Watson, also a former head of the Human Genome Project, reject a faith stand altogether. The worldview a person adopts is independent of the

---

[55] Granville Sewell, *In the Beginning: and Other Essays on Intelligent Design*, 2010, p. 84.

empirical observations and scientific evidence in their field of competence, and depends only on how they interpret that evidence.

Coming to Terms with Billions of Years

In 1543, Nicolas Copernicus died. Following his death, his sun-centered idea of the solar system was published. In it he stated:

> Finally we shall place the Sun himself at the center of the Universe. All this is suggested by the systematic procession of events and the harmony of the whole Universe, if only we face the facts, as they say, 'with both eyes open.'

Today we can update this statement by changing just a couple of words.

> Finally we shall place the Big Bang itself at the beginning of the Universe. All this is suggested by the systematic procession of events and the harmony of the whole Universe, if only we face the facts, as they say, 'with both eyes open.'

Given the reality that the universe may in fact be billions of years old and that common descent is the best explanation of how we came to be, what is the appropriate Christian response? The challenge for the Christian is to be a realist in regard to the evidence in nature without compromising the integrity of faith and the Bible.

How can we grasp the idea of the scale of billions of years of existence? Christian theologian Denis Alexander has suggested that a thought experiment to compress the age of the earth into a twenty-four hour clock may give us an appreciation of the vastness of time.

> So what happens if we start our twenty-four hour clock at zero around 4.6 billion years ago, and imagine that midnight is the present moment in time? Simple forms of life would appear by 2:40 a.m. Single-celled organisms with the beginning of the genetic code flourish by around 5:20 a.m. A long wait ensues until single-celled organisms containing nuclei become visible around lunchtime. A further seven hours passes before multi-cellular organisms start appearing in the sea by 8:15 p.m. The Cambrian explosion where many phyla burst on the geologic scene starts at 9:10 p.m., and in an amazing three minutes an immense diversity of phyla appear, each with a distinctive body-plan. At 9:33 p.m. plants start appearing on land. At 10:11 p.m. reptiles start roaming the land. By 10:50 p.m. the earliest mammals and dinosaurs are appearing, but five minutes later there is a mass extinction at the start of the Jurassic period. Another mass extinction occurs at 11:39 p.m. in which the dinosaurs are wiped out. Not until 11:58 p.m. do hominid precursors appear and a mere three seconds before midnight *Homo sapiens* make their entry. The whole of recorded human history until now is compressed into a blink of an eye, less than one-fifth of a second before midnight.[56]

To heighten the drama, remember that the age of the earth is only about one-third the age of the universe. To reflect the scale of the age of the universe, another three-fold compression is needed.

---

[56] Denis Alexander, *Rebuilding the Matrix*, 2001, p. 345.

Someone has said that if you stretch out your arms in both directions to represent all of earth's history, and someone else scrapes the tip of the nail on your left middle finger with a nail file, you would have wiped out all of human history.

Faced with the concept of this incredible monumental scale, an initial response might be to ponder our insignificance, not only in relation to time but also to the vast spaces of the universe with its innumerable galaxies and their innumerable stars. A person might echo the words of Job 'What are mere mortals that you should make so much of us?'[57]

However as a counter-perspective, Denis Alexander goes on to remind us of the value that God places on human souls.

> If size and time are the main criteria for assessing value and importance, then clearly this objection has some basis. But now let us carry out a further thought experiment. Suppose that the history of our planet was again compressed into twenty-four hours, but this time instead of a linear timescale the scale was set according to the appearance of morality and ethics on the planet. Clearly the picture would look diametrically opposite to the one we had before. This time the complete evolution of life with all its biological diversity would be crammed into almost the entire twenty-four hours for, to the best of our knowledge, no other animals with the capacity for moral choice have ever roamed this planet. And if our planet appears ridiculously small from a physical perspective in comparison with the vastness of the universe, then for all we know if we apply the scale of morality to the universe then our planet

---

[57] Job 7:17.

might look ridiculously large.[58]

Christian biologist Darrel Falk takes a slightly different approach by synchronizing the age of the earth to an earthly year. Even with this expanded scale, recorded human history occurs in the last minute before midnight, and the last hundred years of discovery would be the blink of an eye. But he too reminds us,

> God, however, has given us the privilege – the joy of being able to peer back into time to see the masterpiece unfolding. Let's not close the eyes of our mind to God's work in the past, if only because it may reveal important facets of God's work in the present.[59]

In view of the vastness of time and space now known it may appear that Man has lost his central role in physical cosmology, as stated by the Copernican principle, but that should not be a concern to Christians. In his famous 1973 essay, *Nothing in Biology Makes Sense Except in the Light of Evolution,* Theodosius Dobzhansky said "The earth is not the geometric center of the universe, although it may be its spiritual center."

Why would God waste billions of years to achieve his purpose of creating a being with which he could have a relationship? We have to keep in mind that time is a dimension that we experience like the other three spatial dimensions, except that to us time has a past, present and future component. We have little trouble imagining God being omnipresent, existing everywhere in but not limited to the three

---

[58] Denis Alexander, *Rebuilding the Matrix*, 2001, p. 358.
[59] Darrel Falk, *Coming to Peace with Science*, 2004, p. 133-134.

dimensions of space. God is also omni-temporal, existing in all of time and outside of time. What we perceive as a past, present and future to God is an eternal now. Christian physicist John Polkinghorne says that "God has a relation to time which makes him immanent within it, as well as eternally transcendent of it."[60]

    C.S. Lewis echoes a similar thought. "He, from His vantage point above Time, can, if He pleases, take all prayers into account in ordaining that vast complex event which is the history of the universe."[61] Lewis emphasizes that what we call 'future prayers' have always been in the present to God. The arrow of time limits our present to a single instant, but God somehow sees all of history as happening 'now', so God perceives time entirely differently than we do. We do not have God's perspective of eternity.

---

[60] John Polkinghorne, *The Faith of a Physicist*, 1996, p. 61.
[61] C. S. Lewis, *God in the Dock*, 1970, p. 79.

History of Creation Views

The most extensive ancient commentary on the subject of Biblical cosmology comes from Augustine (AD 354-430). In *The Literal Meaning of Genesis*, he wrote "But at least we know that the Genesis creation day is different from the ordinary day with which we are familiar". His belief, along with other church Fathers of his day like Origen, was that God created everything in an instant, and that Genesis provided a framework to describe His acts of creation and His relationship to His creation.

In general, these writers were writing to affirm the Biblical account in opposition to Greek philosophy (eg. Justin, Irenaeus). It is significant that they wrote long before astronomical, geological and paleontological evidences for the antiquity of the universe, the earth and life itself existed. They stated their positions as being tentative and that the interpretation of the length of the creation days presented a challenge.

Even if the views of the early church fathers were tentative and ambiguous, identifying with their views is not helpful today as they had very little corroborating evidence from nature to support their views. The best we can say is that their knowledge and conclusions were based on Scripture and the world they knew then. Nonetheless, it is very significant that even they were open to and even favoured interpretations other than literal interpretations.

In 1611 the King James Version of the Bible was first published. Thirty-nine years later James Ussher, an Anglican bishop of Ireland used the genealogies recorded in the Old Testament to establish a date for creation - October 3, 4004 BC. This chronology was based on the assumption that they were recorded for historical purposes and that there are no missing generations, an assumption disputed by Hebrew scholarship. Even though Ussher's chronology was subject to dispute at the time by both Bible scholars and critics, it soon began to appear in editions of the King James Bible and for many people became indistinguishable from the inspired passages. This practice would later have a profound effect in America when in 1909 a young Texas preacher named C. I. Scofield produced the Scofield Reference Bible that contained voluminous notes to document the conservative view of the Bible text and the Ussher chronology. This was a brilliant move for the Fundamentalist movement as it combined a partisan interpretation with the Bible text itself, giving it easy accessibility, but also an air of total authority. The notes were presented not as an interpretation of the text but as certain truth, leading some to equate its teaching with God's Word.

The period from about 1650 to 1800 is called the Enlightenment, a period characterized by an emphasis on reason as the primary source for authority and understanding. In the early 1600s, Francis Bacon and Rene Descartes were instrumental in defining a system of thought that came to be known as the scientific method, based on empirical observation and experimentation.

As a result of scientific advancements, more and more of nature came to be explained in terms of natural forces instead of the intervention of God. The emphasis of the scientific method was on empiricism and the use of reason by individuals, with a corresponding reduction of emphasis on religious authority and faith. Isaac Newton was instrumental in identifying laws of nature that defined the behavior of bodies of mass and the forces of energy. He believed that through discovering the laws of physics such as gravity we become more aware of the greatness of God. In 1802, William Paley wrote his *'Natural Theology'*, in which he argued for the existence of God using the argument from design. His audience found it compelling to assume that since the complexity of a watch implies a designer, by analogy the complexity of the universe also implies a designer. The perceived design in nature was often understood to emphasize the beneficence of God. Later Darwin struggled with the idea that God is always beneficent. Even prior to Paley's publication, skeptical philosopher David Hume published *Dialogues Concerning Natural Religion*, in which he showed that the design of the universe does not obviously support the idea of God as presented in the Bible. Toward the end of the 1800s, theology became less of a component of scientific discourse and a strict demarcation between theology and science became common.

Through the 1800s, even the religious establishment became increasingly liberal in their interpretation of the Bible and the 'humanization' or 'secularization' of nature. Through the work of fossil hunters, geologists, and zoologists such as Georges Cuvier and Charles Lyell, it became clear from their calculations of geological deposition rates that life on earth had to be measured in the scale of hundreds of millions of years. In the midst of this controversy, Charles Darwin, a divinity student turned naturalist, published *On the Origin of Species* in 1859. The theory of evolution gained momentum after this publication, primarily because there had never been other credible naturalistic theories.

Contrary to popular belief, most conservative theologians readily accepted an old age for the earth during this time. Notably Charles

Spurgeon preached a sermon entitled *"The Power of the Holy Ghost"* at the New Park Street Chapel containing the following words describing his view of creation:

> In the 2d verse of the first chapter of Genesis, we read, 'And the earth was without form, and void; and darkness was upon the face of the deep. And the Spirit of God moved upon the face of the waters.' We know not how remote the period of the creation of this globe may be - certainly many millions of years before the time of Adam. Our planet has passed through various stages of existence, and different kinds of creatures have lived on its surface, all of which have been fashioned by God. But before that era came, wherein man should be its principal tenant and monarch, the Creator gave up the world to confusion.[62]

Significantly the sermon was preached on July 17, 1855, a full four years *before* Darwin published his *Origin of Species*.

Most people assume incorrectly that Darwin himself was an atheist. His wife Emma was a fervent Christian, whereas Charles Darwin struggled with his beliefs. His discontent with God was likely aggravated by the untimely death of his daughter Anna. He could more accurately be described as either an agnostic or a deist. The final words in his book are:

> There is grandeur in this view of life; with its several powers having been originally breathed by the Creator into a few forms or into one; and that, whilst this planet has gone cycling on according to the fixed law of gravity, from so simple a beginning endless forms most

---

[62] Charles Spurgeon, sermon called *"The Power of the Holy Ghost"*, July 17, 1855.

wonderful and most beautiful have been, and are being evolved.

Although in the first editions Darwin acknowledged the supernatural assistance of God in driving biological evolution, some feel that he did this as a concession to many Christians who were understandably alarmed at the idea of lower life forms developing into more complex life forms, including humans. Ironically, initially many scientists opposed Darwin's ideas, and many theologians agreed with Darwin, especially those in Europe and Britain. Darwin also corresponded frequently with theologians and had their support.

In 1860 there was a widely publicized debate on evolution between Samuel Wilberforce, the bishop of Oxford, and Thomas Huxley, one of Darwin's most vocal supporters, known as Darwin's bulldog. There is considerable controversy about what actually occurred, but the popular recounting states that Huxley humiliated the ill-prepared Wilberforce, and the defeat resulted in Christians being seen as prejudiced, ignorant, in error, deceptive, and in blind opposition to science. These perceptions reverberate to this very day.

German biblical scholar Johann Eichhorn, a contemporary of William Paley, became known as the father of "higher criticism". He, among others, proposed that at least parts of the Old Testament were compiled from late, unreliable documents, and that the Bible's creation account was simply a Hebrew version of borrowed myths. As a result, for those influenced by Eichhorn, faith was severed from fact. Predictably, there was a strong negative reaction to this view of the Bible from the orthodox Christian community.

Origins of Biblical Literalism

How are we to explain the obsession with Biblical literalism that has dominated a large sector of the North American evangelical church in modern times? The origins of this literalistic or young-earth creationist movement are well documented.[63]

Early in the 1900s, a movement known as 'Fundamentalism' arose in reaction to the liberalization of theological views initiated by Eichhorn. 'Fundamentalism' placed a strong emphasis on a high view of Scripture characterized by a rigorous literal interpretation of the Bible. Since the theory of evolution could not be reconciled with this interpretation, it was rejected without any consideration of any supporting evidence and considered totally incompatible with Scripture. Between the years 1909 and 1915, two American laymen, Milton and Lyman Stewart, published twelve small books entitled *The Fundamentals: A Testimony of the Truth.* These books attacked criticism of the Bible and reasserted its literal inerrancy, and carefully defended five basic, essential doctrines of Christian faith, one of which was belief in literal creation and humanity's fall from God's grace in Eden. In 1919, the Fundamentalist movement was organized at a conference in Philadelphia as the World's Christian Fundamentals Association. Unfortunately the opposition to evolution became combative and emotional, and since Ussher's 1673 chronology was the only recognized defense against evolutionism, it was adopted as a necessary doctrine, and the five doctrines became six.

In the last quarter of the nineteenth century, and even in the early years of Fundamentalism in the twentieth, it was rare to find any scientist or Bible teacher who thought the world was only a few

---

[63] Ronald Numbers, *The Creationists, 1992.*

thousand years old and was made in seven literal days. The idea gained momentum in the early twentieth century through the work of Seventh Day Adventist George McCready Price. Price was inspired (as he says) by the words of the Adventist prophetess Ellen White, who insisted that the seven day weekly cycle went back to creation. Price formulated an elaborate alternative geology (although he had no formal scientific training) suggesting that all the strata were laid down in one flood. Ellen White had strongly attacked the early Fundamentalists for not keeping the Sabbath on Saturday and so none of the early Fundamentalists adopted Price's system. Generally the Adventists received little support other than from some Missouri Synod Lutherans.

The debate between evolution and the Bible intensified and peaked in the infamous Monkey Trial of John T. Scopes in 1925 in Tennessee. Scopes was a teacher who willingly allowed himself to be charged with violating Tennessee law against teaching evolution in public schools. The famous atheist lawyer Clarence Darrow defended him. Brilliant orator and three-time presidential candidate William Jennings Bryan provided the Fundamentalist prosecution. Although the judge found the accused guilty and Bryan won the case, the event had a huge negative effect on the cause of Fundamentalism as a result of the testimony in the case and how the media reported the proceedings. Darrow craftily forced Bryan to concede that the six consecutive, twenty-four hour periods of Biblical creation must be longer time periods, with the perceived conclusion that Christians then had no real case against evolutionism. The biased reporting in the case also favoured evolution, and Christians responded by digging in their heels and simply making opposition to evolution one of their core beliefs.[64]

During the first half of the 20th century there was a Fundamentalist tendency to muster pseudo-scientific "facts" to defend the reliability of scripture against Biblical critics in much of the evangelical and Fundamentalist literature, exemplified by people like Harry Rimmer and George McCready Price. These were not credible scientists, but religious leaders who dabbled in science, intending merely to defend a particular view of the Bible or to "prove" the Bible against skeptics. In the preface to *The Christian View of Science and Scripture,* Bernard Ramm lamented that "the noble tradition which was in ascendancy in the closing years of the nineteenth century has not been the major tradition in evangelicalism in the twentieth century. A narrow bibliolatry, the product not of faith but of fear, buried the noble tradition." Ramm's diagnosis applied aptly to men like Rimmer and Price.

The difficulty facing 20th century theologians with a scientific interest was that the practice of science in the modern world necessitated specialization. Indeed, the reward structures in professional science are such that they encourage a deep specialized focus rather than a wide generalized expertise. This makes it difficult for these highly specialized scientists to serve up popularized versions of their knowledge for public consumption, leading to an increasingly wide gap between the professionals and lay people. Added to this difficulty is the fact that twentieth-century scientists were discouraged from allowing their religio-philosophic and scientific dimensions to

---

[64] Edward Larson, *Summer for the Gods: The Scopes Trial and America's Continuing Debate Over Science and Religion,* 1997

inform each other. The tendency of scientists to compartmentalize encouraged them to isolate their practice from their beliefs. In cases where attempts were made to bridge these gaps, the initiative rarely came from the professional side, and when it came from the side of religious scholarship, the attempt came up well short of bridging the gap. As a result, no credible body of literature exists from this time period that attempts to harmonize science with Scripture.

A "no compromise, dig in your heels" brand of Fundamentalist scientific creationism arose in the early 1960's as a response to the Soviet launch of the Sputnik 1 satellite on October 4, 1957. How were these apparently unrelated events linked?

The surprise launch of Sputnik 1, coupled with the spectacular failure of the first two Project Vanguard launch attempts, shocked the United States. In response to Sputnik, NASA was created and the reaction to Soviet superiority led to major increases in U.S. Government spending on scientific research and education. Remember also that Francis Crick and James Watson had discovered the secret of DNA in 1953, and research into human life and related discoveries in life history were exploding. The genetic implications of DNA morphed the traditional view of Darwinian natural selection, common ancestry, and random mutation and adaptation into a neo-Darwinian view that synthesized the heritable aspects of DNA and modern genetic understanding.

Following World War II and with the increasing knowledge of genetics, evolutionary theory was expanded to include a molecules-to-man concept. This development admitted to many shortcomings, especially in explaining the origin of life itself, but in the absence of any other naturalistic explanation, became the established theory that most influenced scientists and educators. The surge in new textbooks with an increasingly naturalistic emphasis alarmed the creationists, and they responded by mobilizing and organizing. One way in which they felt they could gain credibility with educators and textbook writers was to find scientific support for their position.

Young Earth Creationism came into the mainstream in 1961 largely through the book *The Genesis Flood* by civil engineering professor Henry Morris, and biblical scholar J. C. Whitcomb. The book read like a scientific text. It credits George McCready Price and is little other than a rehash of Price's work. It advanced the idea that man and dinosaurs coexisted, and that dinosaurs were wiped out and all fossils laid down in the sedimentary fall-out of the global flood. For many evangelicals who felt threatened by the onslaught of secular science, the intuitive belief that creationism embodied the simple teachings of Scripture became a strong public perception. "Tens of thousands of Christians have been convinced by Morris and Whitcomb's books because *they make sense of the Bible.*"[65]

In 1963 a group of ten Fundamentalist scientists banded together to form the Creation Research Society (CRS) to promote their research. Within ten years this group had grown to 450 members with graduate degrees in science. In 1970 the Creation-Science Research Center (CSRC) was formed to promote the teaching of Young Earth Creationism in high schools. The Institute for Creation Research (ICR) was formed in 1972 to focus on research, education, and public lectures and debates. Unfortunately the view of evolutionism advanced by these organizations equates it to godlessness and immorality, and secular scientists are correctly critical of the activities of these

---

[65] David Watson, quoted in Numbers, *The Creationists*, 1992, p. 338.

organizations being termed 'scientific'. Since 1961 various Young Earth Creationist movements have grown in several countries.

In many ways the quick adoption of Biblical literalism in America is difficult to understand. The early Fundamentalists in the period 1912-1925 had already reasserted the essentials of the Christian gospel without adopting a literalist interpretation – none of the writers in *The Fundamentals* (from which the movement got its name) disbelieved in an ancient earth, and their leading theologians like B.B. Warfield tended to accept a form of evolution. It is understandable that a movement such as the Adventist one, that tends to be both legalistic and literalistic, should give birth to an obsession with literalism, but why should this spread to so many conservative evangelicals? Why did later well-meaning evangelicals adopt principles like "we take the Biblical language literally unless absolutely forced not to"? One factor may have been a reaction to the modern materialist view that only the physical is truly real, and that there is no meaning beyond the physical.

By 1980 the influence of these groups was so pervasive and vocal that their views on creation were thought to represent the beliefs of all Bible-believing Christians. To the secular world, the word 'creationist' implies the young earth position, in spite of the fact that many conservative Christians hold other views. Since 1980, particularly in America, social and political debate has raged on the appropriateness of including evolution and creation science in public school curricula. The antagonism between science and Fundamentalist creationism has been most damaging to any meaningful and constructive relationship between science and Christianity. Mark Noll claims that creation science has damaged evangelicalism by making it much more difficult to think clearly about human origins, the age of the earth, and mechanisms of geological or biological change, "but it has done more profound damage by undermining the ability to look at the world God has made and to understand what we see when we do look."[66] While "they are justified in attacking pretentious claims for science", they "push religious-science negotiations toward the brink of battle.", and "drown out more patient, more careful voices."[67] Noll sees an odd contrast between creationist practice and profession that stunts their ability to perceive the world of nature. Although they profess intellectually to use the scientific method, they do not apply it consistently with respect to Scripture and to nature.

> Under the illusion of fostering a [scientific] approach to Scripture, creationists seek to convince their audience that they are merely contemplating simple conclusions from the Bible, when they are really contemplating conclusions from the Bible shaped by their pre-understandings of how the Bible should be read.
>
> The result is a twofold tragedy. First, millions of evangelicals think they are defending the Bible by defending creation science, but in reality they are giving ultimate authority to the merely temporal, situated, and contextualized interpretations of the Bible that arose from the mania for science of the early nineteenth century. Secondly, with that predisposition, evangelicals lost the ability to look at nature as it was and so lost out on the opportunity to understand more about nature as it is. By holding on so determinedly to our beliefs concerning how we concluded God had made nature, we evangelicals forfeited the opportunity to glorify God for the way he had made nature. In a mirror reaction to the

---

[66] Mark Noll, *The Scandal of the Evangelical Mind*, 1994, p. 196.
[67] Ibid., p. 196

zealous secularists of the twentieth century, evangelicals have gone back to thinking that we must shut up one of God's books if we want to read the other one.[68]

Noll shows that the appeal to a "normal" or "plain" or "literal" interpretation is intuitively attractive to people who believe that any Christian exploration, including scientific exploration, should proceed first from the Bible and then use those conclusions to shape our investigation. The problem is that God's revelation in Genesis is not simple and never has been, and historically has never been approached as simple until the start of the Fundamentalist movement. Noll suggests that creationists should show more confidence in the Bible, and less in themselves.[69]

Just as scientists sometimes have to humbly admit that their explanations are inadequate and need to be refined, Bible believers sometimes have to be humble enough to admit that their interpretation of the Bible falls short and needs to be reformulated. In cases of discrepancies between what we think the Bible states and what science states, Vern Poythress says,

> We must be ready to reexamine both our thinking about the Bible and our thinking about science. We must not assume too quickly that the error lies in one particular direction. In the modern world, we find people who are always ready to assume that science is right and the Bible is wrong. Or, contrariwise, others assume that the Bible is always right and modern science is always wrong.[70]

---

[68] Mark Noll, *The Scandal of the Evangelical Mind*, 1994, p. 198-199.
[69] Ibid., p. 200.
[70] Vern Poythress, *Redeeming Science: A God-Centered Approach*, 2006, p. 43.

He goes on to state that the Bible *is* always right, but it is our *interpretation* of the Bible that may need revision.

Shifting Paradigms

One truth we learn about history is that it repeats itself. We see a certain theory, paradigm or view established as the prevailing way of thinking that best explains reality. As mounting evidences appear to challenge that way of thinking, the counter-arguments to prop up the prevailing paradigm become increasingly onerous and contrived until the entire paradigm collapses under the weight of overwhelming support for a new way of thinking.[71] Aristotle's universe as interpreted by the Ptolemaic view confined the sun and all other planets encircling the earth to concentric spheres. Even after he had hypothesized the revolutionary heliocentric theory, Copernicus felt it necessary to adjust his theory to make the heavenly bodies maintain their circular motions as demanded by the Ptolemaic view. Galileo was forced by the Roman Catholic church to argue that it was only "to save appearances" that Copernicus described his heliocentric theory. The old views did not disappear until Kepler, on the basis of detailed observations, proposed a totally new scheme that did not require circular orbits. Einstein's theory of relativity experienced the same truth-wrenching process. Einstein himself introduced a fudge factor in his equations to conform to his belief in an infinite universe (he was later to describe this as his greatest error). Today we know that these adjustments are unnecessary. That the simpler, more elegant solutions eventually prevail is

---

[71] This concept is often credited to Thomas Kuhn and the development is well described in his *The Structure of Scientific Revolutions*, first published in 1962.

sometimes referred to as the 'beauty principle'. G.K. Chesterton echoed this principle when he commented, "The simplification of anything is always sensational."

In this vein, the physicist Steven Weinberg has written:

> There is reason to believe that in elementary particle physics we are learning something about the logical structure of the universe...the rules that we have discovered become increasingly coherent and universal...there is simplicity, a beauty, that we are finding in the rules that govern matter that mirrors something that is built into the logical structure of the universe at a very deep level.[72]

Albert Einstein followed what he thought to be God's perfect simplicity when he laid out his theory of relativity. After many scientific successes, he reached a dead end when confronted with the unavoidable complexities of quantum mechanics. Each time he read a new modern theory, he rejected it with the words "If I were God, I would not have designed it that way." Eventually fellow scientist Niels Bohr advised him to stop telling God what to do.

The pattern of how our understanding changes when confronted with new information has been well studied in the past half century and can be fruitfully applied to explaining how the Creation Science movement has morphed into the Intelligent Design movement in more recent times. If creation science is the old paradigm of understanding creation held by conservative Christians, the Intelligent Design view may be thought of as the new paradigm. Although it may have its roots in the Creation Science movement, the Intelligent Design movement

---

[72] Steven Weinberg, *Nature* 330, 1987, pp. 433-37

represents a diverse, complex, heterogeneous group that has little in common with the more homogenous Creation Scientist movement, and they are separated chronologically from the beginnings of the Creation Science movement by more than a generation.

An increasing number of Christians in the academic and scientific community emerged during the second half of the 20th century who had historical and philosophical links with the Young Earth Creationists, but were uncomfortable with the Young Earth Creationists' beliefs. Although there are a variety of opinions among those in the Intelligent Design community, in general they, in common with Young Earth Creationists, suggest that each phyla, if not each species, required a special creative act on God's part. While accepting the scientific evidence for the age of the universe and the earth, they were not willing to accept a completely materialistic explanation for the origin and development of life on earth.

Another concept frequently mentioned is 'irreducible complexity', the idea that certain biological systems are designed in such a way that the whole cannot function without all of the parts, and the parts could not have come together without intelligent intervention. The 'fine-tuning' argument, the idea that the universe is uniquely designed to provide a fitting habitat for humans, also plays a part in the thinking of the Intelligent Design group.

In summary, the Intelligent Design advocates differ from Young Earth Creationists in important ways:

1. Although their funding, motivation and leadership is driven largely by evangelical Christian interests, Intelligent Design is a diverse and eclectic collection of personalities and philosophies.

2. They have no particular opinion about the age of the earth, and for the sake of argument accept the orthodox figure of 4.6 billion years.
3. They accept evolution over long ages, but doubt that it can do everything claimed for it by evolutionists.
4. They are open to a non-literal interpretation of the Genesis creation accounts.
5. They do not view a worldwide Noahic flood as central to their understanding of nature.
6. Although they take issue with the boundaries of mainstream science, they accept its legitimacy, and promise "to follow the evidence wherever it leads".

While skeptics in our post-modern society are expressing pessimism over what science can tell us and whether science represents progress in any sense, many Christians are opening their minds to the possibility of science having something legitimate and important to contribute to faith. The Intelligent Design movement represents one recent approach to the question and we pursue our examination of this movement in depth in the next chapter.

Intelligent Design: In the Spotlight

What is ID?

The Intelligent Design movement has captured media attention in the past decade and in some ways bolstered the belief system of many believers. Is this attention and trust well-placed? Considering their reason for being, has the impact of Intelligent Design theory had a negative or positive effect on the Kingdom of God? To try to answer these questions, we can explore the opinions and judgments of the so-called experts in three categories:

1) Proponents of Intelligent Design,

2) Unbelievers who are skeptical of Intelligent Design, and

3) Believers who are critical of Intelligent Design.

The experts whose arguments we review are drawn from a wide variety of disciplines including biology, physics, mathematics, law, education, history, sociology, astronomy, and theology.

Intelligent Design (ID) is a belief system that reacts against an increasingly secular world view that posits ultimate natural causation for all events. Because of the implications of biological evolution for the physical origin and development of humans and the continuity with all life, evolution has come under particular attack by ID proponents. Although ID formally makes minimalistic claims that do not involve theology explicitly, most ID proponents will admit to the theological and metaphysical implications of ID. Since naturalistic evolution challenges the theistic claims for a divine role in the creation of life, ID adopted the strategy of identifying weaknesses in the evolutionary approach to biology, such as the inadequacy of natural selection.

ID was predicated on the failure of the Creation Science movement to make inroads into education through legal recourse, starting with the Scopes Trial of 1925 all the way through to 1987, when the Supreme Court decision *Edwards v. Aguillard* struck down a Louisiana law requiring "equal time" for creationism and evolution.[73]

Intelligent Design has its roots in the design arguments of Natural Theology going back more than two centuries, but has been developed much further with the sophistication brought on by the advance of science's child, technology.

One of the first recorded instances of a statement of intelligent design was made by Alfred Russel Wallace in 1870. He was a committed evolutionist but also a man of Christian faith. When he felt he could not attribute the hairlessness of humans and their large brains to natural causes, he looked elsewhere: "The inference I would draw from this class of phenomena is, that a superior intelligence has guided the development of man in a definite direction, and for a special purpose, just as man guides the development of many animal and vegetable forms."[74]

Even atheist astronomer Sir Fred Hoyle recognized some of the coincidences in nature that support the existence of life. With regard to the special nuclear resonances that cause oxygen and carbon to be produced in stellar nucleosynthesis, he comments "A common sense interpretation of the facts suggests that a super-intellect has monkeyed

---

[73] Details abound in Edward Larson, *Trial and Error: The American Controversy Over Creation and Evolution*, 2003.

[74] Cited in Ruse, Michael, *Monad to Man*, 1996, p. 194 from Alfred Russel Wallace, *Contributions to the Theory of Natural Selection*, 1870, p. 204.

with physics, as well as chemistry and biology, and that there are no blind forces worth speaking about in nature."[75]

Some of the core claims of Intelligent Design are:[76]

1. The scope of science should be extended to allow supernatural explanations.
2. Biological complexity originates from a pre-existing order.
3. Natural selection is limited and therefore macroevolution cannot be explained naturalistically, and thus the origin of species requires a different explanatory mechanism.
4. Nature exhibits patterns that are best explained as the products of an intelligent cause (design) rather than an undirected material process (chance and necessity).
5. Darwinism as a philosophy promotes an atheistic worldview and therefore must be resisted by believers in God.
6. The fine tuning we observe in nature that contributes to the fact of our existence is directly attributable to a supernatural agency.

The claims that cause the most controversy and therefore merit more careful scrutiny are #3 and #4. Because of the sensitive and emotional nature of the theological implications, the debate has often created dissension and division among Christians.

An early ID document defines intelligent design as "a frame of reference that locates the origin of new organisms in an immaterial cause: in a blue-print, a plan, a pattern, devised by an intelligent agent".[77]

Much of the thrust of the Intelligent Design movement is centered in the Discovery Institute in Seattle, Washington, a think-tank started by Howard Fieldstead Ahmanson, Jr., with money inherited from his

---

[75] Quoted in Paul Davies, *The Accidental Universe*, 1982, p. 118

[76] For a general expansion on these points, see William Dembski, *Intelligent Design: The Bridge Between Science & Theology*, 1993.

[77] Ronald Numbers, *The Creationists*, 1992, p. 376.

father's ventures in the banking industry. As a young man, Ahmanson had been influenced by conservative Rousas Rushdoony and Henry Morris, the leader of the Creation Science movement.[78]

In the movie *"Expelled: No Intelligence Allowed"*, Ben Stein tries to make Intelligent Design a cultural issue as well as a political and educational issue. The movie addresses the question of whether the "apparent design" in nature acknowledged by virtually all biologists is genuine design (the product of an intelligent cause and empirically detectable according to the theory of Intelligent Design), or is simply the product of an undirected process such as natural selection acting on random variations. A strong anti-Darwinian bias is evident in the movie.

In addition to criticizing the naturalistic claims of evolution, the *Expelled* movie rejects the notion that "the case is closed" and exposes what it sees as the widespread persecution of scientists and educators who are pursuing legitimate, opposing scientific views to the reigning orthodoxy. A case in point is that of Guillermo Gonzalez who failed to obtain tenure at Iowa State University in 2007. Gonzalez's book, *The Privileged Planet*, coauthored with Jay Richards, although never mentioning Intelligent Design as such, clearly aligns with the arguments. A documentary produced by the Discovery Institute quickly followed the book. Gonzalez and Richards are both senior fellows of the Discovery Institute. Although there was considerable controversy over Gonzalez's failure to obtain tenure, it is difficult to assert that his association with the Discovery Institute had anything to do with the decision. Gonzalez now teaches at an evangelical Christian school in Grove City, Pennsylvania.

---

[78] Ibid., p. 383.

An ironic twist to the movie criticism and the Gonzalez affair is the case of Nancey Murphy, a philosopher at Fuller Theological Seminary, who in 2006 claimed she faced a campaign to get her fired after she expressed her view that ID was not only poor theology, but "so stupid, I don't want to give them my time." Murphy, who accepts evolution, said that Phillip Johnson called a trustee in an attempt to get her fired. Johnson admitted calling the trustee, but denied any responsibility for action taken against her.

From a glance at the Mission Statement of the Discovery Institute,[79] scientific pursuit is not even mentioned. The bottom line theme of the statement is that the Institute is organized as a public relations concern, intent on spreading its vision of renewal through subunits such as the Center for Science and Culture. The defense of its initiatives in education through judicial processes has served to raise the profile of its cause, but the subsequent court failures have been a public setback to the organization and its credibility.

In an internal public relations strategy and action plan document that was later leaked to the public, Johnson described a wedge strategy designed to overthrow scientific materialism, replacing it with a theistic understanding of nature and human beings as God's creation. The long term strategy outlines a three-phase approach: Phase I: Scientific Research, Writing and Publicity; Phase II: Publicity and Opinion-making; Phase III: Cultural Confrontation and Renewal. The strategy

---

[79] "Discovery Institute's mission is to make a positive vision of the future practical. The Institute discovers and promotes ideas in the common sense tradition of representative government, the free market and individual liberty. Our mission is promoted through books, reports, legislative testimony, articles, public conferences and debates, plus media coverage and the Institute's own publications and Internet website". Accessed August 14, 2010 (http://www.discovery.org/about.php).

in the Wedge Document is stated as: "If we view the predominant materialistic science as a giant tree, our strategy is intended to function as a wedge that, while relatively small, can split the trunk when applied at its weakest points."[80] The goal appears to be the insertion of a particular religious view into public schools through cultural indoctrination.[81] The 1999 document explicitly targeted evangelical Christians as the vehicle through which the wedge strategy would be delivered.

What ID Says it is Not

ID does not publicly portray itself as theistic in any way, although most of the proponents of Intelligent Design are Christian. They deliberately go out of their way to avoid ascribing the pre-existing intelligent agency to 'God' or any particular supernatural entity, in deliberate contrast to the earlier Creation Science movement.

ID proponents point out their differences with creation science. With regard to its religious orientation the Discovery Institute states that ID can be differentiated from creation science in the following ways:

---

[80] The full text of the Wedge Document can be found at http://ncse.com/creationism/general/wedge-document.

[81] One long term goal is "to see intelligent design theory as the dominant perspective in science." The longer term goal is "to see design theory permeate our religious, cultural, moral and political life."

1) ID is based on science and withholds science authority from Biblical text, whereas creation science is based on sacred texts.

2) The religious implications of ID are unconnected to ID itself, so ID is officially positioned as agnostic about the nature and methods employed by the Designer(s).

This posturing may be viewed as an attempt to disassociate ID from the Creation Science movement because of the stigma attached to creation science in the secular world. Over the years, creation science overtly portrayed itself in court as a religious movement intertwined with science. This intertwining was what threatened the wall between church and state, and the 1987 *Edwards v. Aguillard* case rejected creation science because it was a religious idea that should not be promoted by government. Although sometimes referred to as 'neo-creationism' by its critics, the Intelligent Design movement arose in response to this ruling, distancing ID from the Creation Science movement.

How did ID get its start?

One of the first writers to galvanize the anti-evolution community after the court reversals in the United States was Michael Denton, an Australian biochemist who wrote "*Evolution: A Theory in Crisis*" in 1985. The book took a fairly technical approach to criticizing deficiencies in the evidence supporting evolution, and was built on an earlier book by chemist Charles B. Thaxton, mechanical engineer Walter L. Bradley and geochemist Roger L. Olsen called *The Mystery of Life's Origin*. This 1984 book attributed the complex origin of life to a divine creator, but the most significant part of the book was its foreword by Dean Kenyon, a professor of biology at San Francisco State University and the coauthor of a major textbook on the chemical origins of life. In the foreword, Kenyon documented his change of mind. He wrote "A major conclusion to be drawn from this work is that the undirected flow of energy through a primordial atmosphere and ocean is at present a woefully inadequate explanation for the incredible complexity associated with even simple living systems, and is probably wrong."[82]

Denton reinforced Kenyon's thought reversal. His book caused a stir among those looking to push back the influence of evolutionary theory in public school textbooks. Denton was an early supporter of the Intelligent Design movement and a fellow at the Discovery Institute. However, in the late 1990s Denton expressed regret that he had used the word *'Evolution'* in his title, indicating that he really intended to criticize Darwinism as a philosophy and not evolution itself. He wrote a further book called *Nature's Destiny* which rescinded his earlier writing, and eventually he disassociated himself from the Intelligent Design movement.

In 1986 Richard Dawkins, ethologist at Oxford University published *The Blind Watchmaker*. This book portrayed evolution as a blind, purposeless process that leaves no room for divine intervention. According to Dawkins, Darwin's work had *"made it possible to be an intellectually fulfilled atheist,"* and he described creationists as

---

[82] Thaxton, Bradley, Olsen, *The Mystery of Life's Origin: Reassessing Current Theories*, 1984, pp. vii, 186.

"ignorant, stupid or insane." The book had a mobilizing effect on the fledgling Intelligent Design movement.

Dean Kenyon and his biology textbook writing partner Percival Davis put their writing skills to work and produced a creationist biology text for high school called *Biology and Creation* in 1989. After the negative Supreme Court decisions on creation science, they renamed their manuscript *Of Pandas and People*, and changed the phrases "creation" and "creationists" to "intelligent design" and "design proponents". Although this editing effort would later come back to haunt them, this was the first document to explicitly promote Intelligent Design.

In 1991 Phillip Johnson, a law professor at UC Berkeley, read Dawkins' book during a sabbatical and became motivated to immerse himself in the study of biology and the history of evolutionary thought to enable himself to critically examine the claims of Dawkins. The result was the manifesto of the Intelligent Design movement, the book *Darwin on Trial*. The book appealed to some because it was critical of 'naturalism' and continued the theme of 'design', but it was the argumentative approach of a legal mind that influenced others to join the cause.

One of the first formal meetings of these like-minded evolutionary opponents occurred at Southern Methodist University in 1992 and featured a debate between Johnson and agnostic philosopher of science Michael Ruse. Other invited speakers were mathematician William Dembski, Michael Behe, a professor of biochemistry at Lehigh University and a Catholic, and philosopher of science Stephen Meyer. Based on the success of this event, Johnson organized a follow-up session at Pajaro Dunes on the California coast in the summer of 1993.

Added to the group at that time were Jonathan Wells, biology graduate student, and Paul Nelson, a philosophy of biology student who was working on a critique of macroevolutionary theory.

This group caught the attention of Bruce Chapman, the director of a Seattle based lobby group devoted to improving transportation and communication in the U.S. Northwest with funding from the Bill and Melinda Gates Foundation. Chapman was a Harvard graduate and a conservative Christian. With funding from the head of Weyerhauser Corporation and the aforementioned Ahmanson, and the encouragement of Stephen Meyer and friends, Chapman created the Center for the Renewal of Science and Culture (CRSC), now known as the Center for Science and Culture, within the Discovery Institute in 1996, dedicated to overthrowing "scientific materialism" and promoting "nothing less than a scientific and cultural revolution."

Michael Behe introduced the idea of 'irreducible complexity' in his 1996 book, *Darwin's Black Box*. Using the analogy of a mousetrap, he identified several biological phenomena that apparently cannot be explained from an evolutionary point of view. Just as a mousetrap fails to function when any part is removed, so an organism like the bacterial flagellum fails to function when any part is removed. The challenge is to explain how a naturalistic evolutionary pathway could have done it.

Another notable book, *Mere Creation: Science, Faith & Intelligent Design*, was published in 1998. The book is a collection of contributions edited by William Dembski from many opponents of naturalism. The contributions resulted from a major research conference held on November 14-17, 1996 in Los Angeles at Biola

University. The project was described as a four-pronged approach to defeating naturalism:[83]

1. A scientific and philosophical critique of naturalism;
2. A positive scientific research program for investigating the effects of intelligent causes;
3. A cultural movement for systematically rethinking every field of inquiry infected by naturalism, reconceptualizing it in terms of design; and
4. A sustained theological investigation that connects the intelligence inferred by intelligent design with the God of Scripture and therewith formulates a coherent theology of nature.

William Dembski, mathematician, philosopher and prolific writer, wrote a book called *Intelligent Design: The Bridge Between Science & Theology* in 1999 that served as both a manifesto of design and an introduction of Dembski's concept of 'complex specified information' and the 'explanatory filter'. According to Dembski, when the odds for a specified event fail to meet the criteria of law or necessity, the only explanation remaining is design by an intelligent mind.

To illustrate Dembski's concept of 'specified complexity', recall the 9/11 World Trade Tower attacks. After the first plane crashed into the first tower, observers thought that a serious accident had taken place. The crash of the second plane into the second tower eighteen minutes later removed all doubt and confirmed that this was a designed event. The result defied all odds and had clearly been specified in advance by the terrorists.

In 2002 Jonathan Wells published *Icons of Evolution: Science or Myth?*, a book designed to cast doubts on Darwinian evolution. Wells, then a biology professor at UC Berkeley and member of the Unification

---

[83] William Dembski, *Mere Creation*, 1995, p. 29.

Church, catalogued alleged frauds and failures from evolutionary history such as Haeckel's embryos, the peppered moths, Darwin's finches, four-winged fruit flies, the Miller-Urey experiment and the inadequate fossil record. The book was highly regarded within the Intelligent Design movement, but severely criticized by the general scientific community.

ID's role in education and the courts

The Intelligent Design movement has had a tumultuous record in the courts, changing strategy from allowing local education board autonomy in choosing curriculum, to lobbying for equal time, to "teaching the controversy". While it is not the intent at this point to document the historical record of the court challenges, it is important to recognize that the judicial involvement is the source of most of the media and public attention on Intelligent Design.

The controversy over the teaching of Intelligent Design theory came to a head in 2005 in Pennsylvania, where the Dover School Board voted that ninth-grade students must be read a statement encouraging them to read about Intelligent Design. A federal judge ruled that the board violated the Constitution in doing so because he thought that Intelligent Design was religious creationism in disguise and that injecting it into the curriculum violates the constitutional separation of church and state.[84]

Recently "academic freedom" bills have emerged but failed in various state legislatures. An "academic freedom" act has been adopted as law in Louisiana, and there is legislation in Florida calling for an "academic freedom" bill that would mandate a "thorough presentation

---

[84] In his ruling, Judge Jones stated "The facts of this case make it abundantly clear that the Board's ID Policy violates the Establishment Clause. In making this determination, we have addressed the seminal question of whether ID is science. We have concluded that it is not, and moreover that ID cannot uncouple itself from its creationist, and thus religious, antecedents." See Edward Hume, *Monkey Girl: Evolution, Education, Religion, and the Battle for America's Soul*, 2007, p. 332.

and critical analysis of the scientific theory of evolution." The pro-evolution National Center for Science Education says such bills are strategies used by creationists to appeal to the American sense of fair play, and give the false sense that there are equally valid sides to scientific issues such as evolution. In spite of many judicial setbacks for the Intelligent Design movement, the issue is still alive.

What do ID proponents say about ID?

Not surprisingly, most Intelligent Design theorists adopt negative statements in an attempt to distance themselves from metaphysical naturalism, as opposed to adopting a positive orientation which would focus on statements defining what Intelligent Design represents.

William Dembski lists the unsolved "utterly intractable" problems still lying at the doorstep of naturalism. In addition to the mutation-selection mechanism, he adds: "the origin of life, the origin of the genetic code, the origin of multi-cellular life, the origin of sexuality, the absence of transitional forms in the fossil record, the biological big bang that occurred in the Cambrian era, the development of complex organ systems and the development of irreducibly complex molecular machines."[85] Sean MacDowell is the son of well-known author and apologist Josh MacDowell. Writing with Dembski in a book targeting high school students, he refers to natural selection as "Darwin's substitute for God."[86]

---

[85] William Dembski, *Mere Creation*, 1995, p. 23. See also William Dembski, *Intelligent Design: The Bridge Between Science & Theology*, 1999, p. 113.

[86] William Dembski and Sean MacDowell, *Understanding Intelligent Design*, 2008, p. 15.

Perhaps one of the biggest obstacles to acceptance within the scientific community is ID's desire to redefine science by expanding the scope of explanations to include supernatural explanations, as stated earlier by Stephen Meyer. MacDowell claims that "Intelligent design does not have to prove that it is a science – it already is a science."[87] In the opinion of Granville Sewell, the majority of scientists today reject ID *a priori* before even evaluating the supporting evidence. ID supporters "claim, quite correctly, that one can deduce the existence of an intelligent designer from the evidence all around us, particularly in biology, but do not attempt to go any further than that, because that is as far as the scientific evidence alone can take us."[88] C. John Collins finds the scope of science as defined by the NSTA[89] to be overly narrow.

> If we insist that "science" can only deal with natural explanations, then we're trying to win by controlling the definitions. Why can't we just say that "science" is "the disciplined and critical study of the world around us"? If we insist that, for some particular historical event, only natural-process-based explanations will count as science, the only way that can be rational is if we already know beforehand that natural factors are the only things involved. But what if we *don't* know that? Then we have no rational right to insist on natural explanations only in science – unless, of course, we're willing to make science independent of the rules of reason.[90]

---

[87] Ibid., p. 41.
[88] Granville Sewell, *In The Beginning, and Other Essays on Intelligent Design*, 2010, p. 121.
[89] See page 10.
[90] C. John Collins, *Science & Faith: Friends of Foes?*, 2003, p. 297.

Collins claims that Intelligent Design adds a legitimate tool-kit for scientific explanations of the natural world by adding the ability to identify design. There are two dimensions of design that he identifies, one is the design of properties and the other is *imposed* design. Science has no problem examining the design of properties. The difficulty with imposed design, which affects the structure and *purpose* of objects, is that *purpose* is something which science cannot deal with. No scientist (including Richard Dawkins) objects to the apparent design in nature. At bottom, the difficulty many scientists have with defining ID as science is the introduction of ultimate *purpose* into the explanatory space of science.

Proponents make some bold claims about Intelligent Design. Do these claims stand up? One such claim made by MacDowell that is also a repeated theme in the move *Expelled: No Intelligence Allowed* is that there is a secular conspiracy to suppress the evidence for intelligent design:

> Intelligent design is so important because the evidence for it is compelling, but Darwinists suppress that evidence to promote a naturalistic worldview.[91]

Is there evidence to support the charge that Darwinists deliberately suppress evidence for Intelligent Design? Only ID proponents seem to sense a conspiracy theory. Still, they put on a brave front and voice their optimism in the promise of their theory. Michael Behe suggests a new world order in the science world is about to begin.

---

[91] William Dembski and Sean MacDowell, *Understanding Intelligent Design*, 2008, p. 29.

> The theory of Intelligent Design promises to reinvigorate a field of science grown stale from a lack of viable solutions to dead-end problems. The intellectual competition created by the discovery of design will bring sharper analysis to the professional scientific literature and will require that assertions be backed by hard data. The theory will spark experimental approaches and new hypotheses that would otherwise be untried. A rigorous theory of Intelligent Design will be a useful tool for the advancement of science in an area that has been moribund for decades.[92]

In Behe's opinion, the ideas of Intelligent Design are on par with those of Newton and Einstein, and just as the discoveries of gravity and relativity rocked their intellectual worlds, Intelligent Design is destined to rock our world. The irreducible complexity concept is one of those ideas.[93]

> Now it's the turn of the fundamental science of life, modern biochemistry, to disturb. The simplicity that was once expected to be the foundation of life has proven to be a phantom; instead, systems of horrendous, irreducible complexity inhabit the cell. The resulting realization that life was designed by an intelligence is a shock to us in the twentieth century who have gotten used to thinking of life as the result of simple natural laws. But other centuries have had their shocks, and there is no reason to suppose that we should escape them.[94]

---

[92] Michael Behe, *Darwin's Black Box*, 1996, p. 231.

[93] Ibid., p. 39. Behe's definition of irreducible complexity is "a single system composed of several well-matched, interacting parts that contribute to the basic function, wherein the removal of any one of the parts causes the system to effectively cease functioning,"

[94] Ibid., p. 252.

Dembski and MacDowell suggest that some personal effort is all it will take to uncover the evidence of which they are so sure.

> Does hard scientific evidence of design exist in nature? If so, can we discover evidence of God's existence? The answer is obvious: Put nature to the test and see where the evidence points. This is precisely what intelligent design does – it has us do the scientific legwork to determine whether a designer actually is responsible for the physical world.[95]

ID advocates argue that for a *natural process by itself* to produce an *informational system* such as the coded DNA message in each human cell is a contradiction in terms. An information system is governed by something outside the components that make it up.[96] Stephen Meyer has produced a long and repetitious book called *Signature in the Cell* that argues that the best explanation for the coded message qualities of DNA is that of intelligent agency. For the study of historical cause and effect, of which the origin of the first cell is one example, Meyer claims that the appropriate approach is one of *abductive* reasoning. Abductive reasoning can be firmly established if it can be shown that it represents the best or only explanation of the "manifest effects" in question. One difficulty with this approach is that there could always be a best explanation, until a better one comes along. Nevertheless, Meyer argues that neither chance nor necessity nor a combination of the two sufficiently accounts for the complexity and quality of the DNA message. He dismisses the many examples of bad design and

---

[95] William Dembski and Sean MacDowell, *Understanding Intelligent Design*, 2008, p. 44.
[96] C. John Collins, *Science & Faith: Friends or Foes?*, 2006, p. 294.

deleterious mutations in genes that result in hereditary diseases and conditions[97] as degradations of originally well-designed DNA. Contrary to all conventional wisdom, Meyer claims that "the vast majority of base sequences on the genome, and even the many sequences that do not code for proteins, serve essential biological functions. Genetic signal dwarfs noise, just as design advocates would expect."[98]

Meyer uses the example of Isaac Newton to make the point that the great scientist was quite willing to endorse intelligent agency for the design he saw in the planetary system.

> Newton suggested that the stability of the planetary system depended not only upon the regular action of universal gravitation, but also upon the precise initial positioning of the planets and comets in relation to the sun. As he explained: "Though these bodies may, indeed, persevere in their orbits by the mere laws of gravity, yet they could by no means have, at first, derived the regular position of the orbits themselves from those laws…[Thus] this most beautiful system of the sun, planets, and comets could only proceed from the counsel and dominion of an intelligent and powerful being."[99]

What Meyer fails to state is that what Newton assumed about the interventional initial positioning was eventually shown to be incorrect

---

[97] For a long list of these fallible and wasteful conditions resulting from deficient DNA, see John Avise, *Inside the Human Genome: A Case for Non-Intelligent Design*, 2010.

[98] Stephen Meyer, *Signature in the Cell: DNA and the Evidence for Intelligent Design*, 2009, p.461.

[99] Ibid., p. 146.

and unnecessary. What Meyer seems to fail to appreciate is that he may be in the same position as Newton.

Thomas Woodward is a professor of the history of science, communication and systematic theology at Trinity College in Florida. In *Doubts About Darwin*, he draws an interesting parallel between the scientific and theological implications of the Big Bang theory, and those of Intelligent Design. Many secular scientists resisted the Big Bang because of the theological implications of creation from nothing, and only came to accept the veracity of the event when the evidence became compelling.

> The Big Bang played a strange role in regard to ID, almost a forerunner...The idea of evidence in nature pointing beyond herself was already bubbling to the surface in the theory Gamow had christened. By the time ID was being formulated in the late 1980s, the Big Bang was cited as highly relevant to design theory in two ways. First, ID theorists observed that the Big Bang was a theory with religious implications, but these implications did not prevent the theory from receiving a fair hearing. *What mattered was whether it was supported by good evidence, not whether it had religious implications.* Likewise, ID theory may have religious implications, but that also should not disqualify it automatically. Second, the Big Bang is one of the first modern scientific theories that provided important scientific hints of true design in the universe. The Big Bang scenario posits a basic *creation event* that naturally raises the question of its own cause. What or who triggered the bang? At a minimum, it seems to *suggest* a designer as one possible explanation, even though it does not necessarily

demand a personal designer.[100]

Does Intelligent Design have the same epistemological depth as the Big Bang theory? Do secular scientists not simply resist, but deliberately suppress Intelligent Design evidence in order to avoid the theological implications?

Intelligent Design theorists need to be held to their commitment to follow the evidence where it leads. When does the evidence become compelling? What are the implications of conclusive evidence? As David Mills says in *Atheist Universe*, "The proof of God's presence would be the greatest scientific achievement of all time. What other scientific finding could possibly compare to proof of God's reality?"[101]

Alvin Plantinga, the American professor of philosophy at the University of Notre Dame, takes a more tentative approach in responding to the claims of Intelligent Design. While admitting that the evidence for God's action in nature can be compelling, he admits that it cannot be conclusive. While alluding to the potential impact this knowledge would have (as in the comment by Mills), he couches his statements more tentatively:

> The claim that God has directly created life, for example may be a science stopper; it does not follow that God *did not* directly create life. Obviously we have no guarantee that God has done everything by way of employing secondary causes, or in such a way as to encourage further scientific inquiry, or for our convenience as scientists, or for the benefit of the National Science Foundation. Clearly we cannot sensibly insist in advance that whatever we are

---

[100] Thomas Woodward, *Darwin Strikes Back,* 2006, p. 157.
[101] David Mills, *Atheist Universe,* 2006, p. 253.

> confronted with is to be explained in terms of something *else* God did; he must have done *some* things directly. It would be worth knowing, if possible, which things he *did* do directly; to know this would be an important part of a serious and profound knowledge of the universe.[102]

The philosopher of science Michael Ruse balances Plantinga's statement by underscoring the idea that science and theology are not an either-or proposition, and that the knowledge gained by the investigation of Intelligent Design would still have to reside on the theological side of the knowledge ledger.

> Even if Plantinga is right, and even if ID theory does give us "an important part of a serious and profound knowledge of the universe," that knowledge is not scientific knowledge. It cannot replace the understanding of life gained through contemporary evolutionary theory.[103]

Intelligent Design theorists make some huge, and many would say impossible claims, and commit themselves to considerable effort to uncover the evidence for these claims. How much progress have they made in the past decade? What impact has the Intelligent Design movement had on the scientific world? Part of the answer lies in the response to the claims of Intelligent Design by the secular scientific community.

---

[102] Alvin Plantinga, Methodological Naturalism, *Perspectives on Science and Christian Faith* 49(3), 1997, 152-153.

[103] Michael Ruse, *The Evolution-Creation Struggle*, 2005, p. 281.

What do unbelieving skeptics say about ID?

As expected, non-believers have not been kind to the Intelligent Design movement. Even the most sympathetic critic, Michael Ruse, refers to the movement as "creationism lite". Other less favorable polemics include the reference to 'IDiots' and Intelligent Design as the equally demeaning 'creation science in a cheap tuxedo'. The quick identification of ID with creation science is likely due to the ease with which the old creationists could be discredited – ready evidence for an old Earth or common descent would quickly quell their scientific arguments, thereby deflecting the critical claims of design.

Michael Ruse labels Intelligent Design not simply as a religious movement, but one that is identified with a narrow portion of American Christians.

> ID theorists insist that one can infer God's existence from the evidence. Hence, even though one cannot properly, without qualification, simply include all of the ID theorists in the creationist camp, one has good reason to see the group as part of this ongoing tradition. It is an American tradition that goes flatly against the secular religion of Darwinism, and does not have a whole lot of time for the proposals of more liberal Christians. As always, the battle is not simply one of fact and truth. It is rather a struggle for the hearts and souls of people, with deep implications for the ways in which we live our lives and regulate our conduct. It is a religious or metaphysical battle, not simply a dispute about scientific theory.[104]

---

[104] Michael Ruse, *The Evolution-Creation Struggle*, 2005, p. 261.

Thus it is not surprising that we see the Intelligent Design movement involved in a political campaign as much as an educational campaign. Michael Shermer was once an evangelical Christian and a creationist who lost his faith in graduate school where Darwin and Genesis were offered as mutually exclusive explanations of origins, and he could not refute the evidence for evolution. His view of Intelligent Design is that it is not just bad science, but it is political maneuvering. The forays into politics by the Intelligent Design movement have been counter-productive.

> The Discovery Institute is about politics, not science. So political, in fact, that the Templeton Foundation - the provider of the largest cash prize available – has withdrawn its support.[105]

So how well does Intelligent Design stack up as a science? Atheist and physicist Victor Stenger points out that most scientists dismiss Intelligent Design not because of the unpleasant theological implications, but simply because it fails to pass the science test. "When scientists express their objections to claims such as evidence for intelligent design in the universe, they are not being dogmatic. They are simply applying the same standard they would for any other extraordinary claim and demanding extraordinary evidence."[106] Stenger is convinced that Behe's training as a biochemist, not an evolutionary biologist, left Behe unaware that mechanisms for producing "irreducibly complex" systems had already been

---

[105] Michael Shermer, *Why Darwin Matters*, 2006, p. 114.
[106] Victor Stenger, *God: The Failed Hypothesis*, 2007, p. 28.

documented six decades earlier by Nobel Prize winner Hermann Joseph Muller.

According to Michael Shermer, ID scores a zero on the science test.

> The fundamental difference between evolutionary theory and Intelligent Design is the nature of explanation: natural versus supernatural. The problem with the supernatural explanations of Intelligent Design is that there is nothing we can *do* with supernatural explanations. They lead to no data collection, no testable hypotheses, and no quantifiable theories: therefore, no science.[107]

He goes on to describe the dilemma Intelligent Design faces should some explanatory device be exposed as accounting for design. Unless that explanatory principle is naturalistic, it is not science, and the supernatural appears to be crowded out even further.

> Even if Intelligent Design advocates are willing to continue searching, what will they do if they discover a new force of nature that accounts for design? How will they identify it? Will it be considered a natural force, or a supernatural force? When electromagnetism and the weak and strong nuclear forces were discovered in the nineteenth and twentieth centuries, scientists did not identify them as supernatural forces; they simply added them to the known forces of nature. If IDers eschew all attempts to provide a naturalistic explanation for life, they abandon science

---

[107] Michael Shermer, *Why Darwin Matters*, 2006, p. 162.

altogether.[108]

David Mills underscores the futility of scientific attempts to uncover the empirical reality of God.

> So if the advocates of Intelligent Design have indeed succeeded in scientifically proving God to be a reality, then I fully expect their Nobel Prize to be forthcoming. Will ID theory actually win a Nobel Prize? The thought is, at the same moment, both sad and amusing.[109]

Mark Perakh is a Russian who spent time in a Soviet gulag for criticism of the former Soviet Union government. He now teaches mathematics at the California State University in Fullerton, California. As an atheist he is critical of Intelligent Design theorists, especially the arguments of mathematician Dembski, which he alleges are pseudo-mathematical.

> Specification, as follows from all Dembski's examples, is nothing more than a *subjectively recognized pattern*. It can be illusory or real, but it has no exclusive status among many factors pointing either to design or to chance.[110]

Neither do Michael Behe's arguments escape Perakh's judgment:

> Attempts to overthrow Darwin's theory, as Behe tries to do, on the basis of often dubious and sometimes even obviously incorrect

---

[108] Michael Shermer, *Why Darwin Matters,* 2006, p. 53.
[109] David Mills, *Atheist Universe,* 2006, p. 253.
[110] Mark Perakh, *Unintelligent Design,* 2007, p. 88.

notions is not a fruitful way to search for truth.[111]

Michael Ruse remains severely skeptical about Behe's one-step (presumably miraculous) concept of irreducible complexity, citing the synergistic nature of selection.

> Behe shows great ignorance of the way in which Darwinian evolution works…generally, such systems are cobbled together from parts that are already functioning in the system and then are turned to other uses.[112]

Intelligent Design proponents point to design when it is convenient and to their advantage to do so, and ignore design when it highlights non-optimal effects. As Ruse describes,

> Note also how Intelligent Design digs a horrendous hole into which fall the designer's good intentions. Many vile afflictions are caused by minor changes at the molecular level. The effects multiply, bringing on lifelong pain and suffering. If the designer is around to make the very complex, why doesn't he take a little time to repair the simple but broken? … The point is made. [ID] is not going to resurrect the argument from design.[113]

ID proponents have countered that evidence of "bad design" may either reveal a less obvious beneficial function, or may be the result of the

---

[111] Ibid., p. 139.

[112] Michael Ruse, *Darwinism and its Discontents*, 2006, p. 282.

[113] Ibid., p. 284.

decay of an original beneficial and rational design.[114] As evidence for this hypothesis is thin, Meyer optimistically includes this proposal as a predication of Intelligent Design.

Michael Behe's own university has taken the unprecedented step of releasing a position statement on evolution and "Intelligent Design", and its relationship with Behe:

> The faculty in the Department of Biological Sciences is committed to the highest standards of scientific integrity and academic function. This commitment carries with it unwavering support for academic freedom and the free exchange of ideas. It also demands the utmost respect for the scientific method, integrity in the conduct of research, and recognition that the validity of any scientific model comes only as a result of rational hypothesis testing, sound experimentation, and findings that can be replicated by others.
>
> The department faculty, then, are unequivocal in their support of evolutionary theory, which has its roots in the seminal work of Charles Darwin and has been supported by findings accumulated over 140 years. The sole dissenter from this position, Prof. Michael Behe, is a well-known proponent of "intelligent design." While we respect Prof. Behe's right to express his views, they are his alone and are in no way endorsed by the department. It is our collective position that intelligent design has no basis in science, has not been tested experimentally, and should not be regarded as scientific.[115]

---

[114] Stephen Meyer, *Signature in the Cell: DNA and the Evidence for Intelligent Design*, 2009, p. 490.

[115] "Department Position on Evolution and Intelligent Design", Department of Biological Sciences, Lehigh University, http://www.lehigh.edu/~inbios/news/evolution.htm, accessed April 11, 2009.

In the closing chapter of *Darwinism and its Discontents*, Michael Ruse identifies the risk of irrelevancy in which Intelligent Design finds itself.

> The Christian has always stressed that despite our great powers, we are limited. We see as "through a glass darkly." Ultimately, all is shrouded in mystery, not to be revealed in this lifetime. Is this not the ultimate betrayal for the Darwinian? Not at all. The Darwinian concurs! The Darwinian has no time for science stoppers or for duds like Intelligent Design. However, Darwinism at base is a scientific theory – you can make metaphysics out of it, but that is not true Darwinism. It cannot – it should not – say everything...Beware of anything that answers everything. It usually ends by answering nothing. And that is certainly not true of Darwinism.[116]

As expected, Intelligent Design theory comes under heavy criticism from writers and scientists in the secular world. Is this because there actually is a secular 'conspiracy' to suppress evidence for Intelligent Design, or is it possible that there are valid concerns about the scientific legitimacy of Intelligent Design? For a less biased opinion, we examine the responses of those in the Christian community that also hold some reservations about the adequacy of Intelligent Design.

What do theistic skeptics say about ID?

The theistic critics of Intelligent Design tend to agree with the non-theistic skeptics that ID is bad science. While the non-theistic skeptics

---

[116] Michael Ruse, *Darwinism and its Discontents*, 2006, p. 209.

are indifferent about the theological status of ID, the theistic critics claim that ID is also bad theology, but they provide the movement with some redeeming value by prescribing some corrective adjustments to how Christians can view the role of God in the natural world.

Authoritative Christian voices critiquing Intelligent Design require qualifications in science or theology, preferably both. Rarely does a single individual combine both qualifications. Examples of exceptions include Alistair McGrath, John Polkinghorne and Denis Lamoureux. However there are many leading scientific experts who also have a strong faith commitment as well as many with a strong theological background who *do* also have a deep understanding of the relevant scientific issues that can speak authoritatively to the issues.

Is it science?

Until the Intelligent Design movement came about, there was very little disagreement in the scientific community, Christian or otherwise, as to what science meant. Laws governed the natural world, and any non-empirical causes were rejected. This is not to say that God is not involved in the natural world, but simply that for our understanding of the natural world we can assume that effects are caused by natural causes, the principle known as methodological naturalism. The Intelligent Design movement attempts to redefine science, carving out an area for itself where criticism is difficult, and charging that methodological naturalism is just a veneer over metaphysical naturalism.

Ted Peters, a Lutheran theologian and Professor of Systematic Theology at Pacific Lutheran Theological Seminary draws some interesting contrasts between the earlier Scientific Creationism and the Intelligent Design movement.

> Scientific creationism accepts the legitimacy of the scientific method while rejecting the interpretation that leads to Darwinian evolution. For the critics of Intelligent Design theory, confining ID within the domain of scientific creationism makes it easier to dismiss ID, since the methodology of science ceases to be at stake. However, Intelligent Design theorists, especially William Dembski, are challenging something more fundamental – the philosophical assumptions of science itself. Notice that Duane Gish and Henry Morris do not challenge the assumptions of the scientific method. Dembski, on the other hand, argues that the method is based on an assumption that does not allow for the existence of purpose as an explanatory device. Perhaps this poses a much more difficult challenge to confront on its own merits. It may be, therefore, that critics want to equate ID with scientific creationism in order to reject it out of hand rather than debate ID claims on common scientific ground.[117]

William Dembski has gone to great lengths to elaborate a methodology for identifying complex specified information. This methodology is meant to be an objective procedure that can be readily accepted by everyone, but in the end the object of putative design must match a pattern in our own mind. Biblical scholar John Walton explains, "When the products of intelligent design are recognized, the process to understand them becomes a historical one, not a scientific one."[118] Try

---

[117] Ted Peters, Hewlett Martinez, *Evolution from Creation to New Creation*, 2003, p. 114.
[118] John Walton, *The Lost World of Genesis One*, 2009, p. 128.

as Dembski might, he cannot escape the reality that our conclusions about design, although compelling, are subjective. Recognizing products of design removes them from the scope of scientific investigation.

Since its inception, the ID movement has failed to establish a beachhead in the scientific community. While pointing out the weaknesses of the reigning evolutionary explanations, ID offers no plausible alternative scientific mechanisms. According to John Walton, ID offers a conclusion in place of a legitimate theory:

> ID does not offer a theory of origins. It offers conclusions from observations in the natural world and posits that those observations argue against the reigning paradigm of Neo-Darwinism. It must be noted, however, that even as many might grant weaknesses in the reigning paradigm, ID would only be one among many alternatives.[119]

Karl Giberson, born and raised in Canada, is an internationally known scholar of science and religion and one of America's leading participants in the creation/evolution controversy. While teaching at Eastern Nazarene College he has taken time to also write several highly regarded books, including *Saving Darwin*. To put Intelligent Design in perspective in the secular world, Giberson states that even if you removed the theological implications of ID, its impact on the scientific world would be minimal.

The publicity surrounding the creation-evolution controversy can

---

[119] Ibid., p. 126.

> easily blind us to the reality that the majority of work in science has absolutely nothing to do with origins and thus couldn't make use of ID, even if it wanted to. Even if the ID approach were fully embraced by the entire scientific community and enthusiastically applied wherever possible, almost nothing would change outside of those small areas of biology and cosmology that study origins.[120]

Additionally, Walton claims that the deliberate choice to be coy about the identity of the designer means that ID theory makes no attempt to interpret Scripture and contributes nothing to theological thinking.[121]

Keith Miller objects to the arguments of the proponents of Intelligent Design not in that they posit design, "but that they restrict its meaning to only certain structures or processes and make it subject to scientific verification."[122] He finds God's design in everything in nature. All creation declares the glory of God. Why, he wonders, should our doctrine of creation be made subject to scientific verification?

> I see no scriptural justification for this. God's creative activity is clearly identified in Scripture as including natural processes. Thus Christians should not fear causal explanations. Complete scientific descriptions of events or processes should pose no threat to Christian theism, unless a person's theology or apologetic has been inseparably welded to an interventionist view of God's actions.[123]

---

[120] Karl Giberson, *Saving Darwin: How to be a Christian and Believe in Evolution*, 2008, p. 160.

[121] John Walton, *The Lost World of Genesis One*, 2009, p. 127.

[122] Phillip E. Johnson and Denis Lamoureux, *Darwinism Defeated?*, 1999, p. 111. Keith Miller writes in response to the debate.

[123] Ibid., p. 110.

Loren Haarsma received a bachelor's degree from Calvin College and a Ph.D. in atomic physics from Harvard University and is currently an assistant professor of physics at Calvin College. Haarsma feels strongly that the modern Intelligent Design movement makes claims that are scientific, philosophical and theological, and that it is important to scrutinize the claims of Intelligent Design in the categories in which those claims are made, and not to conflate the categories with each other. When Intelligent Design makes claims about the irreducibility of biological complexity, this is a scientific claim that should be evaluated on that basis alone. Whether this model has merit determines whether this is good science or bad science. Science asks the following questions, and in so far as Intelligent Design strives to answer these questions, it is scientific:

1) Basis: Can we discover new truths about nature, and if so, why?
2) Processes: What are effective scientific methods for learning about nature?
3) Discoveries: What do we learn about nature when we apply these methods?
4) Inferences: Do scientific discoveries have implications for society, philosophy, religion?
5) Human aspect: What are our motives, ethics, and goals for doing science?

The types of conclusions about puzzling events in nature that scientists can reach, based on models that rely only on known natural mechanisms, can be one of the following:

1) The event is explainable. Good empirical models predict that known natural mechanisms can explain the event.

2) The event is partially explainable. Our empirical models are not sufficiently thorough to explain the event entirely. However, based upon what we know so far, we believe that known natural mechanisms are sufficient to account for the event. We believe that future advances will allow us to explain the event fully.

3) The event is unexplainable via known natural mechanisms. In fact, there are good, empirical reasons for ruling out any model which relies only on known natural mechanisms.

Through building models with improved levels of success, the goal is to move conclusions from #3 to #2 to #1. As long as Intelligent Design restricts itself to these conclusions, it is doing science.

> When advocates of ID try to show that some phenomenon belongs in the category of "unexplainable"—that is, when they attempt to show that conventional evolutionary models which rely only on known natural mechanisms do not match the data in some respects—they are definitely doing science, even under a narrow definition of science. Such arguments might be good, solid scientific arguments, or they might be poorly done, flawed scientific arguments, but they definitely fall into the category of "science."[124]

---

[124] Loren Haarsma, 'Is ID Scientific?', *Perspective on Science and Christian Faith,* Vol. 59, No. 1, Marcy 2007.

Categorically confusing purpose and design

One theologian with a special interest in issues of Darwinism, cosmology and ecology is John Haught, a Catholic Professor of Theology at Georgetown University. According to Haught, Intelligent Design creates an identity crisis for theology as it is forced to answer scientific questions for which it is not suited.

> Unfortunately, many scientifically thoughtful people today are inclined to place theology in an imaginative joust with science. Theological explanation can coexist quite comfortably and non-competitively with scientific explanation. How so? To begin with, theology does not emulate the kind of explanation that science gives with respect to natural causes. Although theology must be conversant with the methods and fruits of scientific discovery, it cannot imitate the scientific way of explaining things without losing its identity. Discourse about divine action, moreover, must begin with metaphor or analogy, or else it is likely to appear as though the notion of divine creativity is competing with scientific accounts of natural causes. A major reason why "Intelligent Design Theory" draws much justified animosity from both scientists and theologians today is that it attempts to situate divine action, barely disguised as "Intelligent Design," in an explanatory slot that is customarily reserved for science. Theology has a legitimate explanatory role in an extended hierarchy of explanations, but it is not an alternative to scientific understanding.[125]

Another well-known and respected scientist and orthodox Christian with similar views is Owen Gingerich. Gingerich was the

---

[125] John Haught, *Is Nature Enough?: Meaning and Truth in the Age of Science,* 2006, p. 59-60.

professor of Astronomy and the History of Science at Harvard University for many years, and made many significant contributions to cataloging celestial bodies as well as becoming the world's foremost authority on Copernicus.

Gingerich begins his argument by stating that there is a legitimate way for Christians to believe in intelligent design, but distances himself from the movement by that name.

> I believe, with the overwhelming majority of Christians, in a universe of meaning and purpose, a universe designed to be astonishingly congenial to intelligent life. Whether we look at the nature and abundance of the atoms themselves or the remarkable ratio of electrostatic to gravitational attraction or the many other details of our physical universe, we know that without these design features we would not be here. In a word, I believe in intelligent design, lower case *i* and lower case *d*. But I have a problem with Intelligent Design, capital *I* and capital *D*. It is being sold increasingly as a political movement, as if somehow it is an alternative to Darwinian evolution. Evolution today is an unfinished theory. There are many questions about details it does not answer, but those are not grounds for dismissing it.[126]

Rather than seeking proofs of divinity through science, Gingerich is content with intimations.

> Intimations of design can offer persuasion regarding the role of divine creativity in the universe, but never proof. Science remains a

---

[126] Owen Gingerich, *God's Universe*, 2006, p. 68-69.

neutral way of explaining things, not anti-God or atheistic.[127]

Gingerich might also have added that science is not pro-God, as Intelligent Design would have us believe. He cites the epistemological failure of ID to distinguish between formal and efficient causes of phenomena, between the 'why' and the 'how'. God fulfills the requirement for *why* we exist; we have been gifted with discerning intelligence to understand *how* we have come to exist.

> There are multiple levels of explanation for any phenomenon. God's role as Sustainer can be described in Aristotelian terms as a final cause, the ultimate teleological reason something happens. Over the years since the Scientific Revolution, however, one vast panoramic scientific picture has been put together that is singularly successful in explaining *how* the universe works, what Aristotle would call an efficient cause. Today scientists, as scientists, play by the rules of a game of coherence, putting together an integrated picture of how things work, without recourse to the miraculous or to ultimate reasons. Essentially, scientists' quest takes place in the realm of efficient causes. Thus, much as I might believe that the universe is best understood in terms of intelligent design, I don't think that would get a spacecraft to Mars.[128]

Gingerich gives further examples as to how ID theory compares unfavorably to other natural causal explanations.

Many leading theorists of ID argue that the evidence for intelligent

---

[127] Ibid., p. 78.
[128] Ibid., p. 73.

input into the evolutionary process is overwhelming. With regard to final causes, those theorists make a good case for a coherent understanding of the nature of the cosmos. But they fall short in supplying any mechanisms to serve as the efficient causes that primarily engage scientists in our age. Intelligent Design does not explain the temporal or geographical distribution of species. Intelligent Design does not help us to understand why Hawaii, in comparison with the older continental areas, has so few species, and why there would be flightless birds on the islands. It does not shed any light on why the DNA in yeast is so closely related to the DNA in human chromosomes. As a philosophical idea, ID is interesting, but it does not replace the scientific explanations that evolution offers. It simply does not offer any insight regarding the numerous related skeletal patterns – for example, the five bones of the coelacanth's fins and the five bones of the gorilla's hand, excellent examples of the sort of mystery illuminated by the hypothesis of common descent with modification.[129]

When it comes to the agenda of the ID movement aiming to revise the science curriculum in schools, Gingerich sees the conflation of primary and secondary causes as a serious problem for ID when he states, "It is just as wrong to present evolution in high school classrooms as a final cause as it is to fob off Intelligent Design as a substitute for an efficacious efficient cause."[130] For this reason he believes "Intelligent Design theorists are making a serious error of category when they propose that Intelligent Design should be taught alongside the theory of evolution in science classes."[131]

---

[129] Ibid., p. 73-74.
[130] Ibid., p. 75.
[131] Ibid., p. 71.

Another area of confusion introduced by Intelligent Design is in the idea that design implies purpose. To John Haught, purpose is a concept that transcends the appearance of design. Design in nature is an adaptive process with no foresight. Purpose is goal-directed and value-laden with a future orientation. To equate purpose and design is to make a category mistake.

> Evolutionary naturalists, along with some religious believers, tend to confuse purpose with "divine intelligent design." And since Darwinism can explain local organic "design" naturalistically some claim there is no need any longer to look for purpose in the universe as a whole. To the pure Darwinian, organisms may seem to be designed, but divine intelligence is not the ultimate cause of their "apparently" purposive features. However, the idea of purpose is not reducible to intelligent design. Design is too frail a notion to convey all that religions and theologies mean when they speak of purpose in the universe. Purpose does not have to mean design in the adaptive Darwinian sense at all.[132]

Howard J. Van Till, who characterizes Intelligent Design as "punctuated naturalism", is troubled when ID confuses purposeful design with the process that executes the design. In Stephen Covey's *Seven Habits of Highly Effective People*, the second habit is "Begin with the end in mind."[133] This habit is based on the principle that *everything is created twice*, first by mental design, then by physical construction. Design implies planning and conceptualizing, whereas assembly involves fabricating and constructing. Conception leads to

---

[132] John Haught, *Is Nature Enough?: Meaning and Truth in the Age of Science*, 2006, p. 101.
[133] Steven Covey, *Seven Habits of Highly Effective People*, 1989, p. 99.

realization. The requirement for intelligence is skewed largely to the design phase, and the assembly phase relies heavily on information. Normal procedure requires that the design be committed prior to the start of assembly. Van Till states that failure to recognize the distinction between design and assembly as the ID literature does "makes it nearly impossible to evaluate each of the two concepts, along with relevant empirical evidence, on its own merits."[134] Perhaps the ID movement could more accurately be relabeled the "Intelligent Assembly" movement!

Steven Barr is a physicist from the University of Delaware who demonstrates that the deterministic and materialistic viewpoint that dominated science prior to the 20th century has largely disappeared, and that science can no longer be reduced to matter in motion, or life reduced to nothing but chemistry.

In his book, *Modern Physics and Ancient* Faith, Barr answers the question "Does Darwin Give 'Design without design'?" by first making reference to Michael Behe's assertion that some cellular processes are "irreducibly complex" and therefore could not have been built up gradually by little steps in a Darwinian manner. Barr sees design not in the natural processes that are the proximate cause of organisms, but in the remarkable laws behind the phenomena. He suggests that Richard Dawkins is myopic in not recognizing the design in the infrastructure required to make Paley's "watch". Dawkins finds the mindless universe successfully crafting astonishing structures by repeated trial and error with what he recognizes as *apparent* design. But Dawkins cannot account for "an immense automated factory that blindly constructs watches, and feels that he has completely answered Paley's

---

[134] Phillip E. Johnson and Denis Lamoureux, *Darwinism Defeated?*, 1999, p. 83.

point. But that is absurd. How can a factory that makes watches be less in need of explanation than the watches themselves?"[135] He concludes that far from disproving the necessity of cosmic design, Darwinian evolution may actually point to it. "We now have the problem of explaining not merely a butterfly's wing, but a universe that can produce a butterfly's wing."[136] As a physicist, Barr acknowledges that the symmetry and order that we can see is based on a deeper and more profound symmetry. It is that order and pattern which he believes points to a designer. Barr avoids the term "intelligent design" because it comes with so much baggage these days, but there is no question that he finds design in the universe at a very profound level.

Reducible complexity

The idea of "irreducible complexity", which could only come from Intelligent Design, is subject to Kenneth Miller's criticism. Miller is biology professor at Brown University after teaching for six years at Harvard University.

> The crux of the design theory is the idea that by themselves, the individual parts or structures of a complex organ are useless. The evolutionist says no, that's not true. Those individual parts can indeed be useful, and it's by working on those "imperfect and simple" structures that natural selection eventually produces complex organs.[137]

---

[135] Stephen M. Barr, *Modern Physics and Ancient Faith,* 2003, p. 111.
[136] Ibid., p. 112.
[137] Kenneth Miller, *Finding Darwin's God,* 1999, p. 135-136.

Francis Collins states that not only does ID make experimental prediction intractable, but some of the predictions of ID such as evidence for irreducible complexity are already in danger of falsification.

> All scientific theories represent a framework for making sense of a body of experimental observations. But the primary utility of a theory is not just to look back but to look forward. A viable scientific theory predicts other findings and suggests approaches for further experimental verification. ID falls profoundly short in this regard. Despite its appeal to many believers, therefore, ID's proposal of the intervention of supernatural forces to account for complex multi-component biological entities is a scientific dead end.[138]
>
> Of even greater significance for the future of ID, it now seems likely that many examples of irreducible complexity are not irreducible after all, and that the primary scientific argument for ID is thus in the process of crumbling. Major cracks are beginning to appear, suggesting that ID proponents have made the mistake of confusing the unknown with the unknowable, or the unsolved with the unsolvable.[139]

Only one demonstrable pathway is necessary to illustrate the intractability of irreducible complexity. Although no proven pathways have yet been shown, plausible mechanisms are suggested by Miller and Collins, leading to the possibility that irreducible complexity is just another open gap in our scientific knowledge.

---

[138] Francis Collins, *The Language of God*, 2006, p. 187.
[139] Ibid., p. 188.

Filling the gaps

Alister McGrath is an evangelical theologian who started his career in molecular biology, but decided to pursue his interest in systematic theology and obtained a Doctor of Divinity degree from Oxford University. After many years of teaching at Oxford (the same university as Richard Dawkins), he took up the chair of Theology, Religion and Culture at King's College London.

From McGrath's perspective, Intelligent Design is moving Christian theology in a dangerous direction, positioning itself in a stance that can be discredited in the future.

> The real problem here, however, is the forced relocation of God by doubtless well-intentioned Christian apologists into the hidden recesses of the universe, beyond evaluation or investigation. For this strategy is still used by the Intelligent Design movement – a movement, based primarily in North America, that argues for an "intelligent designer" based on gaps in scientific explanation, such as the "irreducible complexity" of the world. It is not an approach which I accept, either on scientific or theological grounds. In my view, those who adopt this approach make Christianity deeply – and needlessly – vulnerable to scientific progress.[140]

Of even greater concern to believers, according to Francis Collins, ID theory repeats mistakes of the past, misrepresents who God is and limits our true appreciation for the unlimited creativity of God.

> ID is a "God of the gaps" theory, inserting a supposition of the need

---

[140] Alister McGrath, *The Dawkins Delusion?: Atheist Fundamentalism and the Denial of the Divine*, 2007, p. 30.

for supernatural intervention in places that its proponents claim science cannot explain. Advances in science ultimately fill in those gaps, to the dismay of those who had attached their faith to them. Ultimately a "God of the gaps" religion runs a huge risk of simply discrediting faith. We must not repeat this mistake in the current era. Intelligent Design fits into this discouraging tradition, and faces the same ultimate demise.[141]

The perceived gaps in evolution that ID intended to fill with God are instead being filled by advances in science. By forcing this limited, narrow view of God's role, Intelligent Design is ironically on a path toward doing considerable damage to faith.[142]

ID portrays the Almighty as a clumsy Creator, having to intervene at regular intervals to fix the inadequacies of His own initial plan for generating the complexity of life. For a believer who stands in awe of the almost unimaginable intelligence and creative genius of God, this is a very unsatisfactory image.[143]

C. John Collins, a Fellow of the Discovery Institute, admits that ID is characterized by perceived gaps, but he requires that the type of gaps be carefully defined. "There are gaps, and then there are gaps," he says, where some gaps are due to our ignorance, filled in eventually as our knowledge accumulates. Attributing these gaps to an intelligent agent is a dangerous proposition. In the case of what he calls imposed design, however, a gap exists between what we see and the processes

---

[141] Francis Collins, *The Language of God*, 2006, p. 193.
[142] Ibid, p. 195.
[143] Ibid., p. 194.

we know that might have produced what we see, where it can be demonstrated that no natural process is capable of bridging the gap.

> There is a gap between the message bearing function of DNA and the properties of the chemicals that make it up. There is a gap between human capacities for reason, language, and morality, and what we find in every other animal. From these gaps we conclude that it took some kind of special action, done by an agent, to bridge the gaps.

Demonstrating scientifically the lack of a bridge for the gap is a challenge for the ID movement, and most individuals not associated with the ID movement would not distinguish between the two types of gaps, attributing them all to our lack of knowledge.

Glen R. Klassen, adjunct professor of biology at Canadian Mennonite University, is another Christian who believes that an appeal to perceived gaps is premature and pointless. We have to be careful not to label our ignorance as 'God'.

> When I do science as a Christian, I do exactly the same experiments that would be done by non-theistic scientists. But while they may believe that the laws of nature are godless, impersonal and automatic governors of nature, I am free to believe that they are nothing less than the expression of the faithfulness of God. God is utterly consistent in everything he does. But Intelligent Design proponents want to put biology back into the realm of mystery and miracle. I think that this is premature. There is a good chance that we can see the faithfulness of God even in the evolution of the cell by natural selection. Intelligent Design proponents should be careful not to abandon naturalistic explanations too quickly because

there is good reason to think that God wants the world to be intelligible to us.[144]

An interesting study in contrasts is a comparison between Michael Behe and Kenneth Miller. Both are Catholic, and both are convinced by the evidence for descent of all life from a common ancestor. They differ in their belief of the degree of secondary causality in the evidence. Miller believes the presuppositions and thought development of Intelligent Design create a mental straitjacket.

> As a Christian, I find the flow of their logic particularly depressing. Not only does it teach us to fear the acquisition of knowledge, which might at any time *disprove* belief, but it suggests that God dwells only in the shadows of our understanding. I suggest that if God is real, we should be able to find Him somewhere else – in the bright light of human knowledge, spiritual *and* scientific.[145]

Miller reflects the attitude of biologists in general when he says:

> Is it any wonder that biologists are unable to take intelligent design seriously? Over and over again, the imposition of intelligent design on the facts of natural history requires us to imagine a designer who creates successive forms that mimic evolution. Magicians are master illusionists, and if this magical designer had anything in mind, it must have been to cast the illusion of evolution and nothing else.[146]

---

[144] Glen Klassen, *"Pointing us to a loving God: The paradox of natural selection,"* Canadian Mennonite, May 29, 2006.

[145] Kenneth Miller, *Finding Darwin's God*, 1999, p. 267.

[146] Ibid., p. 99.

The "God-of-the-gaps" accusation is sufficient to point out the inadequacy of Intelligent Design as a theological rationale. Newton and many of his contemporary scientists were committed Christians and had a strong desire to see nature as an act of God. Their discoveries of the laws of nature were understood to reflect God's orderly nature.

> Newton's invocation of God is of interest precisely because of the simple clarity of the reasoning: a solid theory explained many things; the unexplained residue – the explanatory "gaps" – were attributed to God. As science advances, these gaps close. In fact, the closing of such gaps is what we mean by the advance of science. Gaps are the shadows where ignorance hides from the light of science. Inserting God into these gaps has proven, historically, to be a fool's errand and ultimately both unnecessary and embarrassing. Again and again science has made surprising advances that have allowed us to revisit these gaps in our knowledge and, often to our great surprise, close them. Historians of science know this only too well, which may be why this critically important group is so under-represented in the ID movement.[147]

Galileo was familiar with the "God-of-the-gaps" concept. In his *Dialogue Concerning the Two Chief World Systems*, Galileo wrote "It is only in order to shield your ignorance that you put the Lord at every turn." The gaps proffered by Intelligent Design are given names like "irreducible complexity", "explanatory filter" and "complex specified

---

[147] Karl Giberson, *Saving Darwin: How to be a Christian and Believe in Evolution*, 2008, p. 159.

information", but these gaps are subject to the same closure as those identified by Newton and those following him. Giberson explains,

> The doubts that Darwin developed about God's relationship to the natural world troubled him for his entire career. He wanted the traditional view of God as creator to remain intact because of the security that belief provided. He did not want science to be secularized. In the same way, Phillip Johnson, William Dembski, Michael Behe, and their colleagues in the ID movement desperately want God to retain the traditional role as creator, involved in enough of the details to leave divine fingerprints on nature. Like Darwin and the other Victorian mourners at God's funeral, they don't want science secularized. And so they keep fighting the young Darwin's battle for him, picking holes in this or that argument, struggling heroically and with great ingenuity to find examples in nature for which supernatural explanations can still be invoked...The world is a complex place, and there is much about the universe that we still don't understand. We are centuries away from closing the many gaps in our current scientific understanding of the natural world. For a time, perhaps a long time, we may take some comfort in supposing that God hides in those gaps. We can develop ingenious explanatory filters to buttress our confidence that God is in those gaps. But it is the business of science to close gaps, and it has long been the central intuition of theology to find a better place to look for God.[148]

Some ID theorists look at the DNA sequence of bases and see in the coded information the metaphor of a message, equivalent to a computer software program as a set of sequence instructions needed to achieve

---

[148] Karl Giberson, *Saving Darwin: How to be a Christian and Believe in Evolution,* 2008, p. 164.

some end result. A software program can be reduced to a series of bits of 1s and 0s, but it is the particular sequence of the 1s and 0s that constitute a specified sequence to represent information. Is the information in DNA an example of 'specified complexity'? Is there a difference between information, and a message? Haught warns that even this view of the DNA sequence is vulnerable to natural explanation.

> Theology should have learned by now – perhaps the hard way – to avoid seizing territory that may belong more appropriately to scientific modes of explanation. It must not appeal to any "God of the gaps," but instead allow science to push natural explanations as far as these can go – as if God were not a factor – even into the sphere of information. Theology should never give the impression that it has any desire to intrude into, or set itself up as an alternative to, scientific accounts. This means, once again, that the theologian must be suspicious of contemporary anti-Darwinian "Intelligent Design Theory", which has now seized the freshly visible domain of information as an opportunity for inserting the category of "intelligence" into scientific work as an explanatory category. Such a notion will inevitably be taken by most scientists as just one more pointless metaphysical, if not theological, intrusion. Mathematician William Dembski would appear to most scientists to be bringing in a category foreign to science when he accounts for the "specified" informational complexity of DNA in terms of Intelligent Design. If one were to understand intelligent design as the characteristic mode of divine action in nature, such a move, I believe, would be theologically suicidal. After all, the arrangement of genetic sequences does not rule out scientific explanations such as genetic drift or natural selection of random variations in chains of DNA.

Moreover, tying the notion of intelligent design too tightly to specified informational sequencing, risks attributing directly to God not only healthy, but also diseased and "unfit" organisms that result from degenerate DNA chains. This is not a move that a sound theology of nature would wish to endorse.[149]

Denis Lamoureux labels Intelligent Design theorists as "progressive creationists" because they account for the existence of irreducibly complex structures by intervention from outside the normal operation of the universe at some point in history. Such a position can be lost in the light of advancing scientific research. "God appears to be forced further and further into the dark recesses of our ignorance; and yes, the dangerous notion arises that maybe human ignorance is in effect the 'creator', a resident only of our minds."[150] In other words, if God is merely an explanatory stand-in until our increasing scientific knowledge preempts God's explanatory utility, there is no reason to think that the original conception of God's role in our mental environment is not a fabrication.

Aubrey Moore, a Christian defender of Darwin, pointed out the difficulty of this approach in his book *Science and Faith* in 1889 when he succinctly observed that "a theory of occasional intervention implies as its correlative a theory of ordinary absence."[151] Lamoureux adds that Johnson's use of the design argument does not force us to accept a view of life marked by God's direct interventions, but could be evident just

---

[149] John Haught, *Is Nature Enough?: Meaning and Truth in the Age of Science*, 2006, p. 67-68.
[150] Phillip E. Johnson and Denis Lamoureux, *Darwinism Defeated?*, 1999, p. 19.
[151] Aubrey Moore, *Science and Faith*, 2009, p. 184.

as well through a God-ordained and sustained and teleological evolutionary process.[152]

Anti-evolution, anti-naturalism

At a philosophical level, Kenneth Miller finds it ironic that atheistic biologists and Intelligent Design theorists can agree on the materialistic implications of evolution, and yet be so diametrically opposed.

> This clash of two cultures extends over a battle line encompassing every moral, ethical, and legal issue of modern life. The giddy irony of this situation is that intellectual opposites like Johnson and Lewontin actually find themselves in a symbiotic relationship – each insisting vigorously that evolution implies an absolute materialism that is *not* compatible with religion. This means, in a curious way, that each validates the most extreme viewpoints of the other.[153]

Miller takes direct aim at some of the key conjectures of Intelligent Design, giving abundant evidence to refute some of IDs claims.

> The gut reaction of just about any scientist familiar with the evidence supporting evolution would be to answer Johnson's two criticisms head-on. No credible evolutionary sequences? "Those fossil sequences do support evolution, and here are five or ten or twenty examples!" would be the reply. No mechanism? "You've got to be kidding? We can measure the actual rate of morphological change produced in the real world by natural selection, and guess

---

[152] Phillip E. Johnson and Denis Lamoureux, *Darwinism Defeated?*, 1999, p. 26.
[153] Kenneth Miller, *Finding Darwin's God*, 1999, p. 189.

> what? It turns out to be ten to a hundred times *faster* than the amount required to explain even the most rapid transitions in the fossil record!" Johnson's criticisms of historical evolutionary sequences do not hold up under scrutiny, and his charge of a missing mechanism is absolute nonsense.[154]

Denis Lamoureux decries Johnson's lack of understanding of biology. He points out that this follows the pattern of the three leading anti-evolutionists who have shaped the beliefs of the evangelical community, Henry Morris (Young Earth Creationism), Hugh Ross (Old Earth Creationism), and Johnson (Intelligent Design). Their respective doctorates are in engineering, astronomy and law, hardly disciplines relevant to evolutionary biology. Lamoureux argues that Phillip Johnson's knowledge of evolutionary principles and processes is inadequate to the degree that Johnson is not qualified to comment on the science. He congratulates Johnson on pointing out examples where materialism is carelessly imposed on society, but claims that "he overstates his case with regard to the pervasiveness of this philosophical view, and he is simply wrong in suggesting that materialism/naturalism is necessarily associated with the biological theory of evolution or that this dysteleological worldview is universally upheld by the modern scientific community."[155]

Keith Miller laments Johnson's uncritical acceptance of the false equation of metaphysical naturalism with evolutionary theory.

> By accepting that evolution and metaphysical naturalism are inseparable, Johnson allows the atheists to define the terms and set

---

[154] Ibid., p. 91.

[155] Phillip E. Johnson and Denis Lamoureux, *Darwinism Defeated?*, 1999, p. 17.

the agenda of the debate. Evolution becomes an alternative to Christian theism, and the debate is reduced to a choice between undirected, purposeless change and a personal, creatively active God. Our purpose should be to destroy false equalities, not perpetuate them.[156]

Keith Miller argues that this merging of metaphysical naturalism with evolutionary theory inhibits the productive interaction between the sciences and Christian theology.

> To say that scientific and religious statements are fundamentally different is not to say that "religious statements belong to the realm of faith while scientific statements belong to the real of reason". Reason is not limited to science. Our scientific and theological understandings must inform each other if we are to be intellectually whole persons. We must strive toward an integrated Christian worldview that leaves no aspect of human activity or knowledge untouched. Maintaining clear definitions of different types of knowledge actually aids in their integration.[157]

Phillip Johnson urges theistic evolutionists to get leading scientific organizations to "support a new statement unambiguously disavowing the mixing of scientific and religious claims." Keith Miller agrees with this goal, but finds it disingenuous coming from Johnson. "[His] own insistence that evolution is inseparably tied to metaphysical naturalism,

---

[156] Ibid., p. 109.
[157] Ibid., p. 114.

and his efforts to have divine action incorporated into scientific description, are directly in conflict with that stated goal."[158]

ID and metaphysical naturalism find themselves at the extreme poles in the spectrum of views that allow teleological considerations to be included in scientific explanations. Where ID claims that purpose is required to adequately explain irreducible complexity, metaphysical naturalism counter-claims that "even if such an explanation cannot be found, the underlying assumption is that there *must be one* (presumably because all phenomena *must* be the result of naturalistic mechanisms)."[159] Thus both extremes are based on metaphysical premises; "teleology" versus "dysteleology". John Walton concludes that the argument about what kinds of explanations science will allow is largely hypothetical and that the existence of purpose is unaffected.

In a reference to Phillip Johnson's "wedge" document, Lamoureux concludes that the only "wedge" that Johnson is introducing into our society is a wedge between the evangelical church and the modern university. "To conclude, the current popularity of Professor Johnson's antievolutionism in North American evangelicalism is a clear example of this Christian community inheriting the wind."[160]

Johnson's response to this charge is that Lamoureux's evolutionary creationism looks exactly like fully naturalistic evolution to objective observers. Stephen Meyer also insists that "the Creator must do something", must play a scientifically discernible role in the history of life, must "make a difference". "If God's activity remains forever superfluous or undetectable (except through the eyes of faith),

---

[158] Ibid., p. 114.

[159] John Walton, *The Lost World of Genesis One*, 2009, p. 129.

[160] Phillip E. Johnson and Denis Lamoureux, *Darwinism Defeated?*, 1999, p. 45.

then it also becomes scientifically irrelevant."[161] The irony of this situation is not lost on Michael Behe, when he says, "The design of creation, based on physical evidence, is less evident to Denis [Lamoureux] than the design of a neighbor's flower bed, where the design of creation is more apparent to atheist Fred Hoyle than to Christian Denis Lamoureux."[162]

Lamoureux counters by saying that Johnson's philosophy of science leads him to create a sharp dichotomy between "intelligent causes detectable in nature" and "unintelligent natural causes", and sees no tension in the idea that God's action may be scientifically undetectable.

> The unfortunate perception that results from this dichotomous view of nature is that unintelligent causes…appear in a negative light as second- or lower-class operations in creation. But these are in fact ordained and sustained by God to declare his glory in the Creation.[163]

J. P. Moreland is an American philosopher, theologian and Christian apologist, Professor of Philosophy at Talbot School of Theology at Biola University. Moreland is a fellow of the Discovery Institute's Center for Science and Culture and as such is sympathetic to the Intelligent Design cause and critical of the views of theistic evolutionists. In Moreland's view, theistic evolution is functional naturalism that appears to crowd out a place for God to act.

---

[161] Ibid., p. 102.
[162] Ibid., p. 106.
[163] Ibid., p. 67.

If ID theory is bad theology and bad science [according to John Haught], then so be it. What troubles me, however, is that Haught and others who opt for theistic evolution seem to do so with little appreciation for the emergence of scientism in our culture and its impact on people's perception of the availability of theological, ethical, and political knowledge. Theistic evolution is intellectual pacifism that lulls people to sleep while the barbarians are at the gates. In my experience, theistic evolutionists are usually trying to create a safe truce with science so Christians can be left alone to practice their privatized religion while retaining the respect of the dominant intellectual culture. While there are exceptions, many theistic evolutionists simply fail to provide a convincing response to the question of why one should adopt a theological layer of explanation for the origin and development of life in the first place. Given scientism, theistic evolution greases the skids toward placing nonscientific claims in a privatized, make-believe realm in which their factual, cognitive status is undermined. Thus, inadvertently, Haught and those of his persuasion contribute to the marginalization of a Christian worldview.[164]

What is striking about Moreland's view is that he seems unaware of the willingness of evolutionary creationists (not just John Haught) to ask the hard questions, and he seems to prefer a path of safety over a search for truth. Moreland seems ignorant of writers such as Denis Alexander, Denis Lamoureux, Gordon Glover, Bruce Waltke, Peter Enns, Alister McGrath, Ted Peters, Timothy Keller and many others who have engaged in the rethinking of theology in light of historical developments and recent discoveries in science. On the basis of the

---

[164] J.P. Moreland, *Kingdom Triangle*, 2007, p. 45-46.

criticisms of Christian authorities with unfavorable opinions of the science and theology of Intelligent Design, it appears that Intelligent Design itself makes an unnecessary contribution to the misunderstanding of Christianity in the public arena, and may be contributing to the marginalization of a Christian worldview.

Metaphysical / theological implications

Based on the published work of ID advocates, Haarsma finds the *theological* claims of Intelligent Design fall into the following categories:

1) Christians should embrace ID as a way to oppose atheism.
2) The "theistic" part of "theistic evolution" is essentially meaningless.
3) Theistic evolution is dangerous to the Christian faith.
4) God definitely used (scientifically detectable) supernatural events to create biological complexity.
5) It is reasonable to believe that God might have used (scientifically detectable) supernatural events to create first life and biological complexity.
6) Good theology and hermeneutics should lead us to conclude that ID is more likely to be true than theistic evolution.

Haarsma agrees with #5 but finds all the others worthy of debate but seriously flawed.

Publicly, ID refuses in principal to establish or speculate on the identity of the intelligent designer. If the designer is *within* the natural world, then the designer would require a designer, who would also need a designer, and so on to an infinite regress. If the designer is *supernatural*, then by definition the designer is beyond the domain of science. Theologically, the idea of a Designer that occasionally intervenes with acts that contravene natural laws undermines human freedom and makes it difficult to understand the goodness of God, and portrays God as either clumsy or fraudulent. Be that as it may, Haarsma feels that ID is being unfairly criticized for being evasive on the issue of the identity of the designer because ID correctly separates a philosophical question from a theological question. ID simply says that the scientific evidence indicates that the designer was intelligent and purposeful – it cannot determine who the designer was.

Karl Giberson sees a misplaced emphasis by ID on God as designer, to the detriment of recognition of God's other more valuable attributes.

> The God of Christianity has to be way more than just a *designer*. Centuries of Christian reflection on the nature of God have highlighted various characteristics of God: justice, love, goodness, holiness, grace, sovereignty, and so forth. Are not compassion and grace far more central to understanding God than design? Although "designer" can certainly be one of these facets, it takes a backseat to God's other attributes such as love, wisdom and grace.[165]

From his background of both science and religion, Giberson finds that ID falls short on both counts.

> From my perspective, ID must be rejected on two completely separate grounds. In the first place, ID doesn't work scientifically. ID was once [prior to the mid-19th century] a viable paradigm in

---

[165] Karl Giberson, *Saving Darwin: How to be a Christian and Believe in Evolution,* 2008, p. 161.

science, accepted by everyone. But it was *not* abandoned because scientists wanted to get God out of the way, as is so disingenuously claimed by some. ID was discredited because it proved inadequate as an explanation for so many phenomena. In the second place, ID is theologically problematic. To suppose that there are various structures in nature specifically designed by a transcendent intelligence, which we all know is God, is to open a Pandora's box of problems, not the least of which is the problem of bad design. And even when the design is good, what do we make of ingenious designs employed for sinister purposes?[166]

To illustrate his point about bad design, Giberson uses an example lifted directly from Darwin's thoughts about a tiny wasp with a diabolical reproductive process.

> Spotlighting design in nature and attributing it to God raises troubling questions. Nature, as Tennyson wrote, is "red in tooth and claw." And many of those teeth and claws are extremely well designed. Some of them would make it through Dembski's explanatory filter. However, if we run all of nature's marvelous devices through this filter, some uncomfortable results appear. What about the Ichneumonidae, which troubled Darwin? Its remarkable design would certainly make it through Dembski's explanatory filter, and we would have to conclude that the instincts of the Ichneumonidae meet the criteria for ID. So here we have an insect laying eggs inside a caterpillar. The newly hatched parasites live inside the caterpillar, consuming its internal organs. And, in a most amazing illustration of intelligent design, the Ichneumonidae eat the internal organs in a specified order that keeps their host

---

[166] Ibid., p. 156.

> caterpillar alive as long as possible. The parasites are born knowing how to do this; they come into the world with a genetically programmed instinct to consume the internal organs of their host caterpillar in a specific order. Forget blood clotting! This is real design. But it's horrible. I suspect that if the champions of ID were to highlight the most revolting examples of design in nature, the evangelical community would lose all interest.[167]

The idea of diseased and unfit organisms is not necessarily inconsistent with a divine ordering of the natural world. John Haught sees pain and perishing as necessary components of a world that truly enables freedom and love.

> The theological notion of a divinely directed, perfectly ordered world that corresponds to our narrowly human notion of "intelligent design" would be theologically incoherent. The only kind of universe compatible with a God who loves, and who therefore wills the independence of the creation, is one in which contingency is an essential ingredient. And to living finite beings, this contingency can only entail that along with the thrill of being alive there will also exist the possibility of suffering and eventual perishing.[168]

Theodosius Dobzhansky, a noted geneticist and biologist, wrote as a devout Eastern Orthodox Christian. He argued that our conclusions could stem from our knowledge of God's character. He expressed his opinion in the following negatively stated argument:

> Those who choose to believe that God created every biological

---

[167] Ibid., p. 161-162.
[168] Ibid., p. 67-68.

species separately in the state we observe them but made them in a way calculated to lead us to the conclusion that they are products of an evolutionary development are obviously not open to argument. All that can be said is that their belief is an implicit blasphemy, for it imputes to God appalling deviousness.[169]

If we accept that the entrance and existence of life on this world's stage is a purposeful divine act, it seems unnecessary and intellectually irresponsible to invoke further interventions to explain away difficulties in the natural historical record.

Dr. David L. Wilcox is Professor of Biology at Eastern University in Pennsylvania. In examining the genetic evidence, Wilcox, like Kenneth Miller, suggests that we take the evidence at face value, and to not do so casts God in the role of charlatan. Wilcox refers to the frequent Intelligent Design assertion that God employed a "special creation" for each species, and objects that "if God writes fictional narratives into the creation to throw us off, how can we trust either nature or the Word?[170] Carl Zimmer states that all the evidence points to the veracity of evolution, and that "as with previous versions of creationism, Intelligent Design leaves us with a designer who goes to enormous lengths to trick us into thinking that life evolved."[171]

John Haught testified as an expert witness for the plaintiffs in the case of *Kitzmiller v. Dover*. His opinion was that the effect of the intelligent design policy adopted by the Dover School board would "be to compel public school science teachers to present their students in

---

[169] Theodosius Dobzhansky, *Mankind Evolving*, 1961, p. 6.
[170] David Wilcox, *God and Evolution*, 2004, p. 82.
[171] Carl Zimmer, *Evolution: The Triumph of an Idea*, 2006, p. 406.

biology class information that is inherently religious, not scientific in nature." He also testified that materialism, the philosophy that only matter exists, is a belief system, no less a belief system than is intelligent design. And as such, it has absolutely no place in the classroom, and teachers of evolution should not lead their students craftily or explicitly to feel that they have to embrace a materialistic worldview in order to make sense of evolution.

David Wilcox is committed both to a strong biblical faith and to faithful, responsible science. He maintains that there can be no conflict between Scripture and the natural world because God is the author of both.

> The intelligent-design argument usually focuses on the *visible* actions of God, ignoring the possibility that God can act in an untraceable manner. But in fact, the Bible states that God is acting at every point in all space and time. Thus, "God believers" must decide whether an "evident" act is due to God's desire to show his presence, or because he had no other way to accomplish his purposes. On the other hand, for those who have committed themselves by faith to nature's autonomy, the idea of intelligent direction of natural causes is simply incomprehensible (even for those who believe in God). For them, a "god" who acts in nature would be the ultimate intruder in a closed system. Such acts thus would necessarily be foreign elements, not part of nature. As various groups of materialists take up arms on the question of design, they focus on questions concerning how effective independent material mechanisms can be. Are they capable of producing the patterns that we have observed, patterns both in currently living species and in the fossil record? In short, the intelligent-design adherents look for evidence of divine engineering

through material inadequacy, while the "matter worshipers" look for material forces capable of producing complicated and often fascinating results without any outside guidance or purpose. Both searches are driven by much the same motive: piety. This is to say that each seeks to honor the object of worship with apologetics and scholarship.[172]

In an interview, Nancey Murphy explains how Intelligent Design theory fails to acknowledge how God works through nature. As a result, ID theory causes a disconnect between theology and science:

> The intelligent-design movement has the unfortunate effect of promoting the view that science and Christian teaching are incompatible. I leave it to the scientists to get into the details of why ID fails scientifically. The more significant failure is its misunderstanding of divine action. Christians have traditionally understood God to act in at least two ways: by performing special acts (special providence, signs, miracles) and by constantly upholding all natural processes. The ID movement assumes that God works only in the first way. Therefore, to show that God has acted, the ID movement believes one has to identify an event in which no natural process is involved. This is their point in trying to argue that particular events in the evolutionary process cannot be explained scientifically.[173]

To bridge this disconnect, rather than looking for God in events that cannot be explained by natural causes, David Wilcox believes

---

[172] David Wilcox, *God and Evolution,* 2004, p. 46-47.

[173] http://www.religion-online.org/showarticle.asp?title=3310, last viewed April 20, 2009

Christians should learn to see God in the everyday world we see around us.

> But can anyone be sure that there is no intelligence involved in the daily events of nature? We should reconsider the nature of God. A scriptural view of nature assumes that the purposes, plan, and hand of God are behind each situation in space and time. Thus "natural" selection would also always actually be "supernatural" selection.[174]

The God revealed in the Bible is both transcendent to nature, and immanent in nature.

Assessment

"Intelligent Design" has a nice ring to it, and for those looking for a role for God in the evolutionary process or simply in nature as a whole, the objections to philosophical Darwinism appear compelling and are warmly embraced, especially by the non-scientist. However, in the big picture, Intelligent Design is now a fringe activity with little credibility in the mainstream scientific community. Despite the best efforts of the movement, Intelligent Design is not rippling out into the public on waves of scholarly and scientific repute. The criticisms not just of the secular scientific community but also many credible Christian authorities paint ID as a passing fad, already extraneous in the secular world, doomed to irrelevancy. The high profile of the ID movement in its own literature, the media, and the judicial circuit has however caused many in the Christian community to look more seriously into the philosophy of science, the metaphysical implications of design, and

---

[174] David Wilcox, *God and Evolution*, 2004, p. 74.

the relationship between faith and science. Many writers have identified the weaknesses of the Intelligent Design movement, and have suggested remedies to correct our mental environment.

Clearly science is not needed to support faith. Science has never been and is not now a threat to true faith. Evolution, the straw man opponent of Intelligent Design, neither denies nor requires a role for divine intervention.

Intelligent Design confuses formal and efficient (or primary and secondary) causes, and fails to distinguish clearly between methodological naturalism and metaphysical naturalism.

The position taken by ID of not identifying God as the intelligent designer appears to be no more than a ploy to avoid the accusation that the movement is simply a means of avoiding the argument that it represents religion. Its goal appears to be to force schools to include the consideration of an intelligent designer in the teaching of the flawed theory of evolution. However, the flaws in evolution are gradually being overcome as new fossils and genetic pathways are discovered.

There is no evidence that ID represents science as opposed to religion because it cannot claim to be science. As pointed out by Michael Shermer, the supernatural explanations of ID lead to "… no data collection, no testable hypotheses and no quantifiable theories." It is also important to consider the point made by Karl Giberson that ID relates to origins whereas science in general does not focus much on origins; thus, ID has little relevance to the general practice of science.

There is little support for the idea that scientists who support evolution are part of a conspiracy against faith in God. Some have their own secularist agenda, but scientists at large simply interpret data in a logical way; they are led to conclusions about nature because the evidence points in certain directions. If the participation of a supernatural force in nature became overwhelmingly obvious from the data collected, many scientists would admit that God must be involved. However, nature appears to work in lawful, regular and orderly ways that can be predicted from previous experience. From this regularity of nature, we can infer that, as Glen Klassen points out, it appears that "God wants the world to be intelligible to us".

In a secular school setting, incorporating Intelligent Design in the science curriculum is clearly inappropriate. In a Christian school setting, however, it probably would be helpful to inform students of the differences among Young Earth Creationism, ID, teleological evolutionary creationism, and secular evolution so that they are aware of the different ways that the evidence for God's role in creation is viewed among Christians. Students should be encouraged to think critically and to study the writings of various Christian and non-Christian scholars on this subject and decide for themselves what makes the most sense.

In 1870, the British priest John Henry Newman wrote in *A Grammar of Assent*, "I have not insisted on the argument from *design*, because I am writing for the 19th century, by which, as represented by its philosophers, design is not admitted as proved. And to tell the truth, though I should not wish to preach on the subject, for forty years I have been unable to see the logical force of the argument myself. *I believe in design because I believe in God; not in a God because I see design.* Design teaches me power, skill and goodness – not sanctity, not mercy, not a future judgment, which three are of the essence of religion."[175]

---

[175] Italics added, cited in Michael Ruse, *The Evolution-Creation Struggle*, 2005, p. 59.

A Christian with an ideological commitment to Intelligent Design as a faith prop may at this point question whether the prop is necessary at all. One possible response might be "God is not a scientist, and one cannot limit one's search for God to nature". Certainly the Christian can marvel at the wonder and beauty of nature just as the secular naturalist can. Where can one find evidence of God's reality and divine activity? Or, in the words of Carl Zimmer, "Where is God's place if everything does have a natural cause?"[176]

A little reflection should immediately alert us to the recognition that this is a category mistake that fails to acknowledge God's purposiveness and intentions toward us. God's role is not limited to the laws of nature but involves our whole personalities, emotions and attitudes. Keith Ward challenges us to enlarge our view of God.

> In the case of God, the appropriate human relationship is one of worship, awe and gratitude, involving submission and a re-orientation of self. To compare this with the calmly analytic attitude of the scientist in a laboratory is crass. In short, if we see what sort of being God is, we shall immediately see that the experimental method is wholly inappropriate for discerning his being and activity. That is why God cannot occur in any properly scientific account of the world, and why explanations of what happens in terms of Divine action must be different in kind from the explanations of natural science.[177]

The conclusion that Haarsma comes to regarding these philosophical claims is that Intelligent Design offers us a false choice.

---

[176] Carl Zimmer, *Evolution: The Triumph of an Idea*, 2006, p. 382.
[177] Keith Ward, *Divine Action: God's Role in an Emergent and Open Universe*, 2007, p. 82.

The way that ID is typically presented, by advocates of ID, is that we face a choice: either evolution is true or things were intelligently designed. It is evolution or design, one or the other. It is true that some advocates have made the point that this is a false choice. Some advocates of ID have made the following distinction: if biological complexity cannot evolve, then we have detected evidence of intelligent design action in biological history; however, if biological complexity can evolve, that neither proves nor disproves design, it merely means that we cannot unambiguously detect it. That is a very good point, and I am glad that a few advocates of ID have made it. However, that point is not being communicated to most audiences. Most audiences are hearing a very simple message: evolution or design; one or the other. Listen to church members and school boards and scientists. The message they have heard is, "evolution or design, one or the other." Philosophically, that is a flawed choice. Religiously, it is a dangerous message.[178]

Acts of God that are driven by the pressure of Divine purpose may be manifested at pivotal points in the causal chain of natural history, but since God cannot be subject to controlled experiments, these acts do not form part of any scientific explanation. The scientific evidence for complexity, fine-tuning and many other awe-inspiring discoveries of nature can, however, be compelling for those who are open to a rational explanation of the creativity of God. Our exploration continues with the examination of some of these discoveries.

---

[178] Loren Haarsma, 'Is ID Scientific?', *Perspective on Science and Christian Faith,* Vol. 59, No. 1, Marcy 2007.

Common Descent, Common Design, Common Sense

Common descent is the theory that a group of organisms descended from a single progenitor that lived at some time in the past. Sometimes the group is assumed to be all living things, in which case the phrase means that all life originated from a single progenitor that lived billions of years ago. Common descent does not necessarily require that unpredictable mutations and natural selection were the only mechanisms responsible for everything we see in the natural history of life. Other biological mechanisms still unknown to us may also have been in force at various times throughout the evolutionary history of the earth.

Although Darwin's "common descent with modification" is sometimes superficially thought of as synonymous with evolution, there is a subtle distinction. The idea of evolution as gradual changes over time does not necessarily imply common descent. Common descent with modification, however, always implies evolution, including the idea that what is commonly termed "macroevolution" is simply "microevolution" writ large. There is also the implicit idea in common descent that life only originated once on earth or if not, that all other origins are extinct.

A consequence of common descent is that the process can be described as a tree-like graph with branches and twigs representing descendants of earlier branches. In his only diagram in *Origin of Species*, Darwin referred to this branching as the "tree of life".

Conservative Christians traditionally accepted Adam and Eve as common ancestor of all of humanity, but deny any further ancestral relationships between humans and other species. For them, *common design* appears to be the more plausible alternative view. Common design is the belief that the natural world has been intelligently designed, and that the similarities in form and function that we see in organisms have been put there by a Creator. According to this view, God created certain kinds or types, and these kinds share some features deemed good by God for their functioning. Given its common design plan, each species then varies according to the specialization needed for its intended purposes in the natural order.[179] While many who accept common design also accept common descent at *lower* taxonomic levels (species or genera derived from the created kinds), they reject common descent at higher levels. Vertebrates and invertebrates, for example, would not have common ancestors; neither would mammals and reptiles. It is best to examine the evidence and identify which concept provides the better explanation of the natural world before making a rational choice between the two.

When Charles Darwin composed the book for which he is most famous, *On the Origin of Species*, he based it on nearly a lifetime of collection, reflection and observation of nature. The internal debate that consumed him early in his professional career was whether there was a continuity of living organisms produced by a history of "transmutations", or whether a divine agent had intervened to create each species in a miraculous way. The question expressed itself as an external debate between the catastrophists, who believed that the earth had experienced massive upheavals each of which introduced new life forms, and uniformitarians, who held that the natural processes that we

---

[179] Thomas Fowler and Daniel Kuebler, *The Evolution Controversy*, 2007, p. 116.

see in place today could explain everything we observe in nature.[180] Although the catastrophists represented the traditional and majority view at the time, the uniformitarian views of geologist Charles Lyell were to play a large role in convincing Darwin of the sufficiency of natural processes, enough for Darwin to conclude that "We must, however, acknowledge, as it seems to me, that man with all his noble qualities . . . still bears in his bodily frame the indelible stamp of his lowly origin."[181]

In Darwin's mind, the question was settled in what he called "descent with modification". Although he did not fully understand the actual source of modification or the means of heredity, he correctly assumed that offspring varied somewhat from their parents but inherited many of the parental attributes. Natural selection as the primary mechanism of evolution explained common descent to Darwin's satisfaction.[182] Common descent was seen to be contrary to the view of common design, a view held by many of Darwin's older and respected contemporaries, especially those with theological backgrounds. Not wishing to offend the contrary view of many of his friends, Darwin withheld release of his opus until 1859 when forced to publish by the impending release of the same thesis by Alfred Russel Wallace.

Darwin's key arguments were based on the fossil record and morphology, the similarity of comparative anatomy distributed through time and across geographical regions. These arguments were not sufficient to convince many of his contemporaries, but they did gain

---

[180] Michael Ruse, *Charles Darwin*, 2008, p. 4-5.
[181] Charles Darwin, *The Descent of Man*, 1871, p. 619.
[182] John Gribbin, *In Search of the Double Helix*, 1985.

strength over the years as Darwin's earlier twin assumptions were confirmed. Because of Gregor Mendel and his pea-breeding experiments, the genetic basis of inheritance was discovered. Later researchers like Thomas Hunt Morgan using studies of fruit flies showed that variation in the genetic makeup of organisms was due somewhat to mutations caused by chemical or radioactive damage, but largely by genetic copying errors.

The discovery of the genetic code shortly after 1953, when Francis Crick and James Watson found the double-helical structure of DNA, revealed that life is based on a genetic "alphabet" of four nucleotides that serve as the letters. These four nucleotides are correspondingly assigned the letters A, C, G, and T which represent the four nitrogenous bases inside the nucleotides that make up DNA: adenine, cytosine, guanine, and thymine. The four character alphabet was found to form three letter words, where each word is used to specify a corresponding amino acid. Twenty different amino acids can be assembled into proteins in unlimited combinations to produce all the enzymes and other proteins used to sustain life. All of life, from amoebas to birch trees to cats to humans, is based on this common genetic triplet code (see section on Genetics). Furthermore, many of the genes encoded in the DNA of different life forms are very similar, and in many cases identical. The question then arises as to what better explains this amazing discovery, common descent with modification, or common design by an all-wise God? And if organisms are produced by unbroken law and not by divine fiat, are we to infer that a naturalistic position is the best explanation? And finally, if we adopt a naturalistic position, does it necessarily diminish the role of a divine Creator and "miracles", or even make a divine Creator unnecessary?

In the following sections each of the main areas of evidence for common descent and common design will be examined in order to form a basis from which to draw conclusions. Although we can never be guaranteed, the evidence strongly suggests that God used the natural process of common descent to guide the development of life. If that is the case, what does that infer about common design?

Morphology

It is appropriate to begin by examining the evidence that Darwin had at his disposal. Darwin saw striking novelty when he examined the basic body plan of vertebrates, yet he also saw a highly conserved architecture in the vertebrate limbs. He found that in spite of a variety of diversified fins, wings, legs, paddles, flippers and hands over a great range of sizes, every terrestrial vertebrate limb was built on a variant of the five-digit limb at the end of two short parallel bones extending from a large single bone. The cat, whale, bat and human all demonstrate this characteristic bone structure, each adapted to its own requirements. Although the structure of the bat wing is entirely different from that of a bird wing, this is to be expected, as a bird is not a mammal. Darwin pointed out "What can be more curious than that the hand of a man, formed for grasping, that of a mole for digging, the leg of the horse, the paddle of a porpoise, and the wing of the bat, should all be constructed on the same pattern, and should include the same bones, in the same relative positions?" The similarity of features, or homology, of not just the vertebrate limb but also many other body structures demonstrated to Darwin the validity of common descent.

Opponents of common descent point to the architectural similarity of body parts as evidence of common function drawn from a common design, somewhat like car designers attaching the same wheels or transmissions to various cars. Intuitively, we should then expect similar patterns of construction, such as we see in all vertebrates. Later we shall see where there are difficulties with this approach.

Not much has changed in the area of morphology since Darwin's day, other than its close relationship to genetics, which we explore in more detail later.

Paleontology

One of Darwin's chief concerns in support of his thesis was the inadequacy of the fossil record in his day. He noted that "in all the vertebrate classes the discovery of fossil remains has been a very slow and fortuitous process", and candidly admitted "I do not pretend that I should ever have suspected how poor a record of the mutations of life the best preserved geological record presented, had not the difficulty of our not discovering innumerable transitional links between the species which appeared at the commencement and close of each formation, pressed so hardly on my theory." Optimistically he voiced hope that the gaps in the record would be filled in to vindicate his postulates. Prior to Darwin, people accepted gaps in the fossil record as genuine, reflective of the Creator's intention to introduce new species through time. As Darwin's thesis became accepted, the gaps were increasingly seen by his supporters as products of incomplete fossilization as organisms evolved, reflecting a metaphysical intellectual shift from supernaturalism to naturalism.

As the process of natural selection became better understood, the gaps in the fossil record could be explained as the result of *stasis*, a long period of geologic time where there was little environmental pressure to cause organisms to adapt. Some species could be identified in the fossil record over hundreds of thousands of years. In fact some species alive today, like the lake sturgeon, are known as 'living fossils' because they have no close living relatives and from their fossil record they appear not to have changed over millions of years. When the environment changed, due to events like climate change, mountain and island formation, asteroid impacts, ice ages, and continental separation, other existing species rapidly (in geological time) adapted to these ecological niches, in some cases evolving into new species. Stephen Jay Gould and Niles Eldredge became well known for naming this interpretation of the fossil record as "punctuated equilibrium".

The past 150 years have seen major gaps in the record filled in, strengthening the weak link that troubled Darwin. Evidence for reproductive, single-celled, life goes back beyond 3.5 billion years. In the post-Cambrian period after 540 million years ago, hard body parts first appear in the fossil record. Intermediate fossil links between two living forms can be found, suggesting that these (or some distant relative) then evolved into today's forms. The forms of life ranging from the more primitive to the more advanced forms are found in roughly progressive geological layers of older strata to newer strata respectively. Darwin recognized this as he states: "The inhabitants of each successive period in the world's history have beaten their predecessors in the race for life, and are, in so far, higher in the scale of nature; and this may account for that vague yet ill-defined sentiment, felt by many paleontologists, that organization on the whole has progressed." When J.B.S. Haldane was asked which discovery could possibly *disprove* common descent, he reportedly replied, "Fossil rabbits in the Precambrian!" Clearly no Precambrian rabbit fossils or any other anachronistic fossils have ever been found in rock strata where they were not expected.

One transitional fossil known to Darwin was *Archaeopteryx*, a crow-sized reptile bird first discovered in Germany in 1860.[183] This creature from 145 million years ago had bird-like features, like feathers, a wishbone, and wings, but it had more in common with theropod dinosaurs, with features like jaws with small teeth, a long bony tail, and separate fingers on the wing. Ten fossils of this species have now been discovered, the most recent one in 2007.

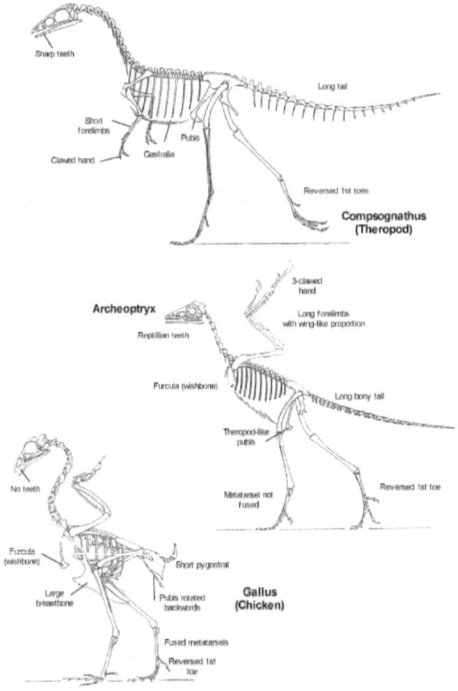

Figure 2. Comparison of skeletal structure of Archaeopteryx with ancient theropod (top) and modern chicken (bottom).

---

[183] Jerry Coyne, *Why Evolution is True*, 2009, p. 40.

In the 1990s, a whole parade of bird-like feathered theropod dinosaurs was discovered in lake sediments in China. These creatures are dated more recently than *Archaeopteryx* by about 10 million years, and show clear evidence of well-preserved early feathers. As the fossil dates become more recent, the fossils show greater similarity to modern birds. The reptilian tail shrinks, the teeth disappear, the claws fuse, and a larger breastbone appears to anchor the flight muscles.[184]

The ancestry of the horse family is richly documented in fossil sediments in North America starting from about 55 million years ago.[185] The range of fossils spans sizes from some no larger than house cats up to today's horse, and includes about three dozen extinct genera and a few hundred different extinct species in all. Surprisingly all modern species of horse including donkeys and zebras fall within a single genus, *Equus*, indicating that all but one branch of the horse family tree has been pruned by extinction. Differences in characteristics of species that went extinct appear to be linked to climate and food source changes.

As the fossil history of horses in North America was being revealed, T.H. Huxley observed the progression from an early four-toed species to the present day one-toed horse, and predicted that further back in the record there would be a five-toed horse. To his satisfaction, a short time later just such a fossil (*Eohippus*) was found.[186]

Whales, dolphins and porpoises have been recognized as mammals since the seventeenth century. A whale is warm-blooded, feeds milk to young that are born live, and has hair. The closest living

---

[184] Ibid., p. 44.

[185] Kenneth Miller, *Only a Theory*, 2008, p. 47.

[186] Michael Ruse, *Charles Darwin*, 2008, p. 115.

relative to a whale is a hippopotamus. Whales retain rudimentary vestigial hind legs and a pelvis. How did whales end up in the ocean? A history of this process has emerged in the last twenty years through the discovery of a chronologically ordered sequence of fossils that shows their movement from land to water. These fossils belong to a 10 million year time span beginning 52 million years ago. Over that period of time this group of animals underwent dramatic changes, including increased size, reduced hind legs and pelvis, and more highly developed flippers, all consistent with adaptations to the aquatic life.

One of the most dramatic fossil discoveries of recent times came in the Canadian arctic in 2004. Neil Shubin from the University of Chicago predicted that a transitional form between early lobe-finned fish and four-footed vertebrates (tetrapods) would be found in rock strata around 375 million years old. Until 390 million years ago, the only fossil vertebrates that could be found were fish, and by 360 million years ago tetrapod fossils first appear. It was expected that the transitional form, if it existed, would be found in a geological environment such as Ellesmere Island. After five years of searching on Ellesmere, Shubin's team hit pay dirt.[187] In an ancient streambed they found what they called *Tiktaalik*, a fossil that retains characteristic fish features such as gills, scales and fins, but also has amphibian features such as a flattened head like a salamander with eyes and nostrils on top, more robust fins, and a neck. *Tiktaalik* is thought to be an evolutionary branch, if not a direct link, between earlier fish and later amphibians.

---

[187] Jerry Coyne, *Why Evolution is True*, 2009, p. 37.

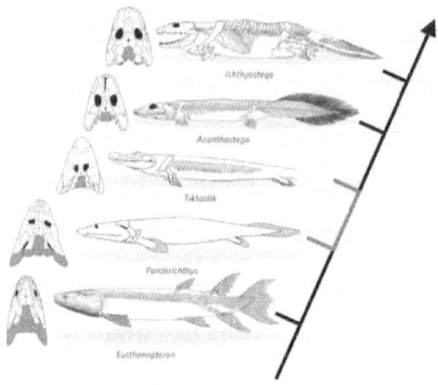

Figure 3. Sequence of fossil discoveries showing gradual changes from fish to amphibians.

Darwin had very little to say about the human fossil record, as at that time there was very little evidence to point to, but he did promise that "light will be thrown on the origin of man and his history." In the last thirty years or so, this promise has been abundantly fulfilled.[188]

Evidence for more than a dozen distinct human-like species has been found in different areas of Africa, dating from the last five million years.[189] Additionally several species have been discovered in China and East Asia, filling out a large tree of possible pre-human ancestors. These hominoid fossils show increasing bipedalism and brain size through the ages, traits which distinguish humans from the rest of the great ape family. Very few if any of the hominoid fossils may be direct ancestors of modern *Homo sapiens*; they may represent extinct branches on the tree that have evolved from the stem that led to today's

---

[188] Kenneth Miller, *Only a Theory*, 2008, p. 92.

[189] Jerry Coyne, *Why Evolution is True*, 2009, p. 190.

human family. For example, the several dozen Neanderthal specimens that have been found likely represent an extinct branch of European hominids.

Given the sheer improbability and unpredictability of fossilization, fossil evidence is psychologically convincing for many people, but for others it is just a marginal piece of corroborating evidence. Remarkably, intermediate forms are always found in the expected rock strata reflecting the correct temporal sequence, sandwiched between the forms that came prior and the forms that came later. Gaps still remain in the fossil record. Recent fossil finds have been able to partially fill these gaps. Is the evidence strong enough to support *Archaeopteryx* and *Tiktaalik* as transitional species in a naturalistic sequence? Do the stories of the whale, the horse and humans illustrate common ancestry, or is common design a better explanation, with each individual species in the genera just an enhanced model similar to how each year's new car model improves on the previous year?

Biogeography

One of the strongest aspects of Darwin's "one long argument" was the one related to biogeography, based largely on his personal experience of navigating the globe for five years on the *Beagle*. Biogeography relates the geographic distribution of living animals and plants, as well as the relationship of living organisms to the fossils in the same geographic location. Aside from the limitations in the fossil record, the biodiversity of fossils and living forms in the same regions is plainly visible for all to see, and Darwin summed up his findings with the words: "In each great region of the world the living mammals are closely related to the extinct species of the same region."

Several observations about biogeography call for an evolutionary explanation. Similar ecological niches or climatic conditions do not necessarily have similar life forms. For example, although North and South America have similar matching ecological zones, the organisms within those zones are markedly different. Variances in organisms also occur across barriers. The life forms in Australia, isolated by ocean, are different from life forms elsewhere. Where there are no barriers across an ecological zone, life forms in all parts of the zone resemble each other. An obvious conclusion based on these observations is that organisms tend to radiate throughout an ecological zone unless restricted by geographic barriers like water or mountain ranges, and adapt and diversify within their ecological niche. Each life form appears only in places where they have been able to go and adapt to the conditions there, and they are restricted from places where they cannot go.

Sometimes the "barrier" is simply the presence of other life forms that already occupy an ecological niche. An example that illustrates this is Wallace's Line in the East Indies. In 1876 Alfred Russel Wallace observed that a division marks two separate groups of inhabitants of the many islands on each side of the line between Bali and Lombok. Inhabitants on opposite sides of the line are quite different even though the closest islands are only 20 miles apart and quite similar ecologically; inhabitants on the same side, though separate, are similar. Birds on Bali are "western" and are related to birds on Java and Sumatra, while birds on Lombok are "eastern" and related to those of Papua New Guinea and Australia.

Speciation in action can also be observed in the case of "ring species". These are related, linked populations that circle a geographic area where adjacent groups within the ring interbreed but the end groups have diverged genetically and hence do not interbreed. The geographic area can be as small as a mountain valley or as large as the globe. A species of salamanders, the Ensatina salamanders, form a ring around the Central Valley of California. Another example of a ring species is the greenish warbler complex in Asia. A ring of six sub-species interbreed, except for two groups in the region where the two extending arcs of the ring are about to rejoin. In this area the two sub-species present behave like different species with different songs and no interbreeding.[190]

A classic example of ring species is the circumpolar species "ring" of *Larus* gulls around the Arctic Circle. The Herring Gull, which lives primarily in Great Britain and Ireland, can hybridize with the American Herring Gull, (living in North America), which can also hybridize with the Vega or East Siberian Herring Gull, the western subspecies of which, Birula's Gull, can hybridize with Heuglin's gull, which in turn can hybridize with the Siberian Lesser Black-backed Gull. The last is the eastern representative of the Lesser Black-backed Gulls back in north-western Europe, including Great Britain. The Lesser Black-backed Gulls and Herring Gulls are sufficiently different that they do not normally hybridize; thus the group of gulls forms a continuum except where the two lineages meet in Europe.

---

[190] Michael Ruse, *Charles Darwin*, 2008, p.123.

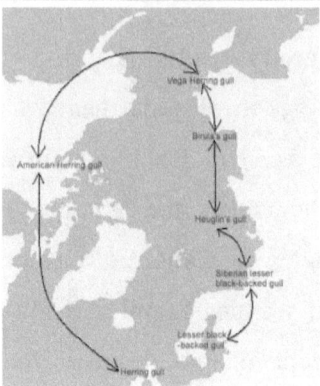

Figure 4. Circumpolar ring of species of *Larus* gulls.

The continent of Australia provides an outstanding "laboratory" for observing common descent in action. Australia has similar ecological niches to other parts of the world, yet because Australia has been isolated from the rest of the globe for a long time; those niches have been filled by different life forms but the Australian and non-Australian species have converged, showing amazingly similar adaptations to those niches.

Where placental mammals have taken over certain zones in much of the rest of the world, similar marsupial mammals have taken over similar niches in Australia. There are grassland grazers such as the kangaroo, tree-dwelling leaf-eaters such as the koala, burrowing carnivores such as the marsupial moles, and hunting carnivores such as the quoll. These species are all significantly different from each other, but all are marsupials. Christian authors Loren and Deborah Haarsma ask "Why would all these different ecological niches be filled by marsupials in Australia and nearby islands and by placental mammals everywhere else? Common ancestry can explain it."[191]

Christian biologist Simon Conway-Morris has strongly advocated the concept of convergence, the idea that the evolution of life forms is constrained by the ecological environment in such a way that we can expect different species to fill out these niches in similar creative ways. Thus there are striking similarities between the extinct South American

Figure 5. Strikingly similar features of marsupial and placental mammals that existed in different ecological niches.

marsupial thylacosmilids and the extinct North American placental saber toothed cat, each filling a niche for cat-like predators with shearing/stabbing weapons. Conway-Morris claims that there is a certain inevitability of adaptation for a given environment that results

---

[191] Deborah Haarsma and Loren Haarsma, *Origins: A Reformed Look at Creation, Design and*

in a similar biodiversity if the evolutionary tape could be played back repeatedly. He goes so far as to say that "if humans had not evolved then something more-or-less identical would have emerged sooner or later."[192] He explains that "the recurrent tendency of biological organization to arrive at the same 'solution' to a particular 'need' leads to the conclusion that the emergence of human intelligence is a near-inevitability."[193]

Fossil evidence suggests that at one point South America also had a significant marsupial population of various species. Most of these have since become extinct, but an explanation for the presence of marsupials in Australia is based on the fact that South America and Australia were part of the same land-mass more than 200 million years ago.

The discovery of plate tectonics and the resulting continental drift strongly suggests that at one point the earth consisted of a single land mass, known as Pangea, which slowly broke apart. Support for this hypothesis comes not just from the geological similarities between the edges of existing continents, but also from the biogeographical distribution of fossils.

Evolution, 2007, pg. 166.

[192] Simon Conway Morris, *Life's Solutions: Inevitable Humans in a Lonely Universe*, 2003, p. 196.

[193] Ibid., p. xii.

Figure 6. The ancient land mass of Pangea, showing demarcations where modern continents formed their boundaries.

The oldest marsupial fossils are actually found in North America dating back to around 80 million years old. After spreading southward into South America and flourishing there, they reached the southern tip around 40 million years ago. The earliest Australian marsupial fossils are 30 million years old, indicating a migration through Antarctica, which was still joined to South America and Australia at that time. This hypothesis was strong enough to suggest to scientists that marsupial fossils could be found in Antarctica, and sure enough, in 1982 they found more than a dozen species of marsupials on Seymour Island, right on the pathway between South America and Australia. The fossils had the expected age as well, between 35 and 40 million years old.[194]

For example, *Lystrosaurus* is a mammal-like reptile that is short, fat and squat, not the prototype of a world traveller. Yet its fossil distribution includes parts of Africa, Asia and Antarctica. Not surprisingly, at the time the *Lystrosaurus* existed in the Lower Triassic, these continents, according to the continental drift theory, would have all been connected.

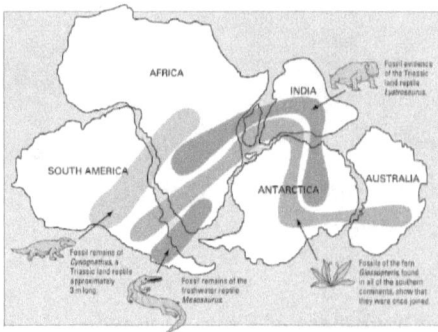

Figure 7. Shows how the radiation of various species, including *Lystrosaurus*, can be explained by the close proximity of modern continents in ancient Pangea.

A more complex example that illustrates a historical pattern of immigration and extinction is the examination of the fossil patterns in North and South America. Michael Ruse explains,

> Home-grown North and South American mammals are significantly different. However, in the fossil record there are North American forms in South America – and some of them, or their descendents, are still extant in South America – and conversely some South American forms in North America – with corresponding extant forms. These are not very old fossils; they go back about 10 or 12 million years, with a large jump in migration about three million years ago. The reason is now obvious. North and South America were parts of different land masses, which – thanks to continental drift – moved closer together and about three million years ago

---

[194] Jerry Coyne, *Why Evolution is True*, 2009, p. 95.

joined up along the Panamanian land bridge. Before the land bridge formed, when the continents were close together, some mammals moved from island to island across the gap, and then with the join there was a real rush.[195]

To South America:

Bears
Camels
Cats
Dogs
Elephants
Horses
Peccaries
Rabbits
Raccoons
Skunks
Tapirs
Weasels

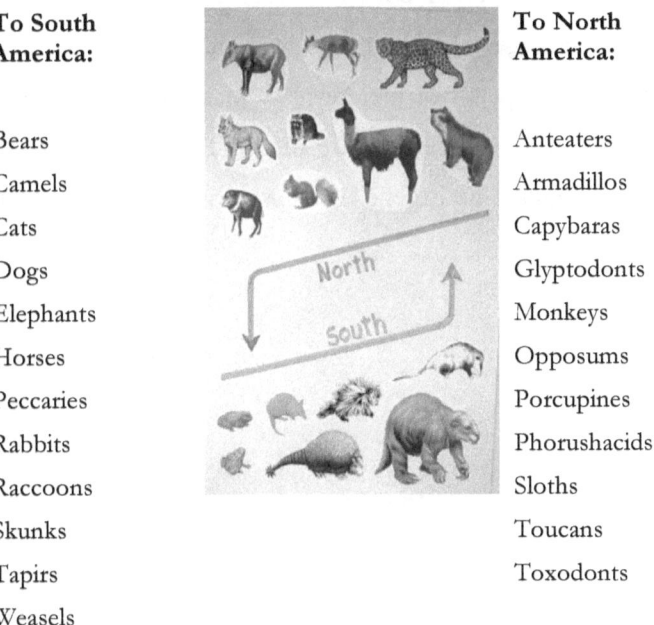

To North America:

Anteaters
Armadillos
Capybaras
Glyptodonts
Monkeys
Opposums
Porcupines
Phorushacids
Sloths
Toucans
Toxodonts

Figure 8. Various life forms that are thought to have migrated between North and South America around three million years ago.

The migrating life forms still alive today represent those species that successfully adapted to their new environments and diversified within those ecological niches.

Biogeographical patterns can also be observed in the genetic distribution of humans. Sickle cell anemia is a genetic disease that

---

[195] Michael Ruse, *Charles Darwin,* 2008, p. 130.

afflicts African Americans in particular. When both copies of a recessive gene exist in a child, it has insufficient or deformed (sickle shaped) red blood cells and often dies. Surprisingly, when there is only one copy of the recessive gene, the blood cells are normal but now they confer some resistance to malaria. As a result, the defective gene survives because natural selection does not weed it out as long as it affords a survival advantage. In Uganda where malaria is endemic, there is a high correlation between incidence of sickle-cell genes and the incidence of malaria. This geographic distribution pattern of the defective but helpful sickle-cell gene is most easily explained in evolutionary terms.

Embryology

Embryology is one of the most dramatic recent contributors to providing new information about evolutionary development at the earliest stage of organic life. Although the technology was not developed in Darwin's day, the study of embryos was an important area of study for him and some of his contemporaries. The German Ernst Haeckel in particular was famous for illustrating the similarity of early stage embryos for life forms as different as adult frogs, chickens and humans. Haeckel's publication in 1874 came well after Darwin's *On the Origin of Species* in 1859 and even after *The Descent of Man* in 1871, but Darwin was influenced by similar thinking of the earlier Karl Ernst von Baer, another German known as the father of embryology. Haeckel's "biogenetic" law: "ontogeny recapitulates phylogeny" stated that the embryo went through stages of development that reflected the evolutionary adult stages of the life form itself, with the early gills and tail reflecting a fish-like state. The concept he was promoting was well known at the time, but this particular formulation has been discredited by modern biology. However, there are numerous connections between embryological structures and the stages of those structures in evolutionary terms. Jerry Coyne describes below how modern biology has now substantiated this general idea, using the human circulatory system as an example.

Darwin confessed that the study of embryology gave him much pleasure and increased his confidence in his picture of development, and under Baer's influence Darwin noted the connection between embryos in the present and the fossil record of the past. "As the embryonic state of each species and group of species partially shows us the structure of their less modified ancient progenitors, we can clearly see why ancient and extinct forms of life should resemble embryos of their descendants, - our existing species."[196]

Even human embryos show evidence of this link with the past. Jerry Coyne illustrates the evidence in the case of the furry human fetus, contrasting our status as "naked apes" with other primates.

> Around six months after conception, we become completely covered with a fine, downy coat of hair called *lanugo*. Lanugo is usually shed about a month before birth, when it's replaced by the more sparsely distributed hair with which we're born. Now, there's no need for a human embryo to have a transitory coat of hair. Lanugo can be explained only as a remnant of our primate ancestry: fetal monkeys also develop a coat of hair at about the same stage of development. Their hair, however, doesn't fall out, but hangs on to become the adult coat. And, like humans, fetal whales also have lanugo, a remnant of when their ancestors lived on land.[197]

Embryology today is known as evolutionary development ("evo-devo"), and recent years have seen the most incredible and unexpected findings that not only underscore Darwin's estimation of the importance of this area, but also establish the link between DNA and the finished organism.[198] While homologies like the forelimb in morphology link all vertebrates, molecular homologies link organisms as different as humans and fruit flies!

---

[196] Charles Darwin, *On the Origin of Species*, 1859, p. 449.
[197] Jerry Coyne, *Why Evolution is True*, 2009, p. 80.

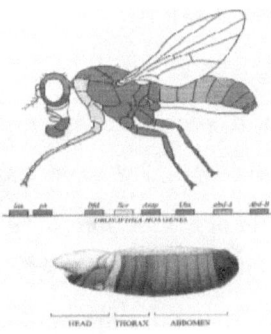

Figure 9. Fruit fly (*Drosophilia*) and fruit fly larva, showing sequence of HOX genes with body plan.

Genes that regulate the identity and order of body parts are called "homeotic genes". They tell the embryo where to put an eye and where to put a leg. A subclass of homeotic genes called the "HOX genes" appear in all bilaterally symmetric organisms. In the fruit fly (*Drosophila*), a mutation in a homeotic gene might cause a body part to appear where it does not normally appear. With some deliberate or accidental manipulation, an extra set of wings may appear, or a leg may sprout from where an antenna should be. Further research into these master control genes revealed that they exist on a single chromosome, and are arranged in the exact order in which they are expressed in the fly, first the head, then the thorax, and finishing with the abdomen. Even more surprising was the finding that HOX genes are also found in other bilaterally symmetric organisms, including humans, performing analogous functions to those in fruit flies. Instead of a single HOX cluster, humans have four clusters, each on a different chromosome and

---

[198] The total constitution of the DNA of an organism is its genotype; the form of life expressed by those genes is referred to as the phenotype.

each controlling the development of a particular segment of the developing human body. Each human cluster is a close match for the HOX gene in the fruit fly.

It appears that the core process of genetic development has been conserved over billions of years. The same basic process is performed through the master regulatory function of the HOX genes and the homology between the DNA genes of *Drosophila* and all other bilaterans, including frogs, fish, mice and humans.

We know that the copying process of a cell's DNA is a high fidelity operation, with built in error detection and correction. However, each copying cycle still introduces 100 to 200 copying errors, which may seem like a lot but pales to insignificance when considering that the human DNA has over three billion base pairs.[199] There is built-in robustness in the genetic triplet code. Code redundancies, multiple triplet codes that specify the same protein, imply that genes can sustain mutations at a single base pair and still continue producing the same proteins (see section on Genetics). Given the predominance of non-functioning base pairs in the genome, odds are that copying errors will occur in the non-functioning sections of the genome, resulting in no functional change in the operation of the cell. Most remaining errors are neutral, lethal, or somewhere in between, but any other errors must be considered as "successful mistakes" that provide the rich raw material of natural selection, the variations that make the diversity and complexity of life possible. Natural selection provides the context within which these "successful mistakes" are conserved and inherited, and damaging mistakes are weeded out.

---

[199] Mark Ridley, *Mendel's Demon*, 2000, p. ix.

The key regulatory proteins that form the basic biochemical machinery in each cell to control their own growth and division are shared in all living cells. These proteins interact with each other to determine the timing of when a cell will copy its genetic information and when it will divide to form two cells. These key proteins are almost identical in all life forms, from yeast to sea urchins to humans. These core components are reused in flexible and different ways. Some people feel that the genetic code has been adapted to facilitate variation, to promote change, to select for "evolvability". Marc Krischner and John Gerhart describe this view in a recent book:

> Central to our argument is that these [core] processes, many of which have been conserved for hundreds of millions or even billions of years, have very special characteristics that facilitate evolutionary change. They have been conserved, we suggest, not merely because change in them would be lethal (although that might be a factor), but because they have repeatedly facilitated certain kinds of changes around them. Many of the conserved core processes have the capacity to be easily linked together in new combinations. New linkages can occur with a minimum requirement for genetic change and hence can happen readily. A new combination of processes can arise with little or no change of the units themselves.[200]

In other words, where core processes have been preserved in evolutionary development because they provide a framework for beneficial facilitated variation, such systems have proved to be more evolutionarily fit in the long run.

---

[200] Marc Kirschner and John Gerhart, *The Plausibility of Life*, 2005, p. 35.

> Instead of a brittle system, where every genetic change is either lethal or produces a rare improvement in fitness, we have a system where many genetic changes are tolerated with small phenotypic consequences, and where others have selective advantages, but are also tolerated because physiological adaptability suppresses lethality.[201]

Owen Gingerich points to the curious case of "six finger dwarfism" among his highly inbred Amish relatives in Lancaster, Pennsylvania. About seventy-five cases of offspring with six fingered hands were identified, half of them stillborn, all of them traceable to an immigrant couple from 1750.[202] Gingerich's point is not to say that the six fingered dwarfs are an evolutionary advance, but to illustrate how quickly mutations in regulatory genes can make fundamental design changes to an aspect of an organism.

Developmental biologist Sean Carroll makes a couple of points about the implications of these fundamental discoveries and the realization that organisms seem to have a genetic toolkit for producing *variation*, the raw material for evolutionary change.

> First of all, this is entirely new and profound evidence for one of Darwin's most important ideas – the descent of all forms from one (or a few) common ancestors. The shared genetic tool kit for development reveals deep connections between animal groups that were not at all appreciated from their dramatically different morphologies. Second, the discovery that organs and structures that were long viewed as independent analogous inventions of different

---

[201] Ibid., p. 226.

[202] Owen Gingerich, *God's Universe*, 2006, p. 63.

animals, such as eyes, hearts, and limbs, have common genetic ingredients controlling their formation has forced a complete change in our picture of how complex structures arise.[203]

In the view of Christian biologist Kenneth Miller, this modular toolkit optimized for segment-by-segment development was refined over hundreds of millions of years and offers a ready explanation for what appears as an "explosion" of body plans in the Cambrian period 540 million years ago.

> The earth's first multicellular organisms, which appeared in the Ediacarian period as much as 100 million years before the Cambrian, had to evolve a way to deal with all those cells. It took millions of years, but eventually they developed a system of switches that could activate alternate programs of development in different parts of the body. This enabled them to lay down an anterior-to-posterior axis, and then to switch on one program of development to produce the head, another for limbs, another for the abdomen, and another for the tail. This revolutionary development was so powerful that it led to the explosion of body plan experimentation that characterized the Cambrian period, and the successful experiments gave rise to the major animal groups that persist to this very day.[204]

There are other lessons that we can learn from embryology. Jerry Coyne describes the embryonic development of the circulatory blood system.

---

[203] Sean B. Carroll, *Endless Forms Most Beautiful*, 2005, p. 285.
[204] Kenneth Miller, *Only a Theory*, 2008, p. 130.

Our blood vessels go through especially strange contortions. In fish and sharks, the embryonic pattern of vessels develops without much change into the adult system. But as other vertebrates develop, the vessels move around, and some of them disappear. Mammals like ourselves are left with only three main vessels from the original six. The really curious thing is that as our development proceeds, the changes resemble an evolutionary sequence. Our fishlike circulatory system turns into one similar to that of embryonic amphibians. In amphibians, the embryonic vessels turn directly into adult vessels, but ours continue to change – into a circulatory system resembling that of embryonic reptiles. In reptiles, this system then develops directly into the adult one. But ours changes still further, adding a few more twists that turn it into a true mammalian circulatory system, complete with carotid, pulmonary, and dorsal arteries.[205]

We are left with a number of observations:

1. All vertebrates, each with a different adult form, begin development looking like a fish embryo.

2. Mammals form their heads and faces from embryonic structures that have the same appearance as the structures that develop into the head and gills of fish.

3. Vertebrate embryos go through a contorted sequence of changes in their circulatory system that do not resemble their adult form until the final stage, with the prior stages roughly mimicking the order of vertebrate ancestors (fish to amphibian to reptile to mammal).

---

[205] Jerry Coyne, *Why Evolution is True*, 2009, p. 75.

A similar tale can be told with respect to our kidneys and fingers. The human embryo actually forms three different types of kidneys in sequence, with the first two discarded before the final kidney appears. The transitory kidneys have similarities with those of jawless fish and reptiles, respectively. The fingers on our hands start off as webbed appendages but then the cells between fingers are programmed to die by a process called "apoptosis".

While Coyne admits that it is just a hypothesis, he suggests that the "adding new stuff onto old" principle is at work, a process that causes one developmental program to be added on top of an existing one. Development is a very conservative process, and it is usually safer and more efficient to tinker with an existing system than to remodel one from scratch. Such remodeling might result in all sorts of adverse side effects in the formation of other structures. "To avoid these deleterious side effects, it's usually easier to simply tack some less drastic changes onto what is already a robust and basic development plan. It is best for things that *evolved* later to be programmed to *develop* later in the embryo."[206]

In many ways then, embryology points to the continuity of all of life, continuity not only with all other existing life today but also with all of life in the past.

Genetics

One of the most remarkable discoveries following the discovery of the helical structure of the DNA molecule itself was the fact that all of life,

---

[206] Jerry Coyne, *Why Evolution is True*, 2009, p. 78.

from bacteria to tea leaves to elephants, shares the same genetic toolkit. The four base molecules, adenine (A), cytosine (C), guanine (G), and thymine (T) appear in a specific sequence in each gene and combine to define the order of amino acids in the construction of proteins. Each amino acid is specified by a sequence of three consecutive bases. For example, if the base sequence of GCT is read, the amino acid alanine is selected and added to the composition of the protein, while if the sequence GGA is read, the amino acid glycine is added. According to the central dogma, so named by Francis Crick, genetic information flows from DNA where it is stored, is transcribed to RNA, and transferred to ribosome molecules where it is translated to transform the nucleic blueprint into protein. The RNA "alphabet" uses the three bases adenine, cytosine and guanine, but substitutes uracil (U) for thymine.

The triplet code can be compared to the Morse code, where a different sequence of dots and dashes each represent a different alphabetic letter.[207] Thus dash-dash-dot might represent the letter 'G'. Some authors have recognized another parallel in the modern world by comparing the genome and its architecture with computer programming and data storage and manipulation.[208]

This triplet coding is highly conserved almost without exception throughout all organisms. This surprising molecular unity is what makes it possible to put human genes into bacteria (for example, to

---

[207] Richard Colling, *Random Designer*, 2004, p. 60.
[208] See for example Dennis Bray, *Wetware: A Computer in Every Living Cell*, 2009, and David Goodsell, *The Machinery of Life*, 2009.

produce recombinant insulin) and fly genes into mice and have them function correctly.[209]

		Second letter			
		U	C	A	G
First letter	U	UUU, UUC } Phe UUA, UUG } Leu	UCU, UCC, UCA, UCG } Ser	UAU, UAC } Tyr UAA Stop UAG Stop	UGU, UGC } Cys UGA Stop UGG Trp	U C A G
	C	CUU, CUC, CUA, CUG } Leu	CCU, CCC, CCA, CCG } Pro	CAU, CAC } His CAA, CAG } Gln	CGU, CGC, CGA, CGG } Arg	U C A G
	A	AUU, AUC, AUA } Ile AUG Met	ACU, ACC, ACA, ACG } Thr	AAU, AAC } Asn AAA, AAG } Lys	AGU, AGC } Ser AGA, AGG } Arg	U C A G
	G	GUU, GUC, GUA, GUG } Val	GCU, GCC, GCA, GCG } Ala	GAU, GAC } Asp GAA, GAG } Glu	GGU, GGC, GGA, GGG } Gly	U C A G

Figure 10. Genetic code table showing triplet codes of nucleotides that map to the twenty amino acids used to specify proteins.

There is a level of redundancy built into the coding scheme. Twenty amino acids are used almost exclusively to create all proteins needed for life. With an 'alphabet' of four letters, it is possible to form 64 (4x4x4) three letter words called codons, but only 20 words (ie. amino acids) plus a few punctuation marks (stop codons) are needed. The spare triplets are used as synonyms so that one amino acid may be specified by more than one triplet. This is called code degeneracy. Several amino acid triplet codons show *fourfold degeneracy*, meaning that only the first two bases are required to specify the amino acid and

---

[209] Thomas Fowler and Daniel Kuebler, *The Evolution Controversy*, 2007, p. 101.

the third acts as a wildcard.[210] This common genetic toolkit indicates that there is a high degree of continuity in all of life on earth.

Another development indicating a surprising level of commonality is the degree of similarity in genomes of different species. Comparative genomics is a field that has exploded in the last decade. Entire genomes have been sequenced, including the human genome in 2002. The most unexpected finding is that organisms share a high level of genetic structure. Because of the high degree of similarity of the mouse and human genomes, genetic testing in mice is often directly applicable to better understanding of the human genome. Recent DNA sequencing has revealed that roughly 95% of the entire human genome can be aligned directly with the chimpanzee genome. At the level of the genes themselves, there is more than 98% overlap between the human and chimp genomes.[211] The human cytochrome *c* protein is exactly the same as the chimp protein and the human gene for encoding the cytochrome *c* protein, made up of 104 amino acids, is approximately 1 per cent different from chimpanzees, 13 per cent different from kangaroos, 30 per cent different from tuna fish and 65 per cent different from that in the fungus *Neurospora*.[212] Examining the amino acid sequence of cytochrome *c* and the redundancies in the nucleic bases required to synthesize that amino acid sequence reveals

---

[210] Nick Lane, *Life Ascending: The Ten Great Inventions of Evolution*, 2009, p. 47.

[211] Chimpanzee Sequencing and Analysis Consortium, "Initial Sequence of the Chimpanzee Genome and Comparison with the Human Genome," Nature 437 (2005): 69-87, H. Watanabe et al., "DNA Sequence and Comparative Analysis of Chimpanzee Chromosome 22," Nature 249 (2004): 382-388.

[212] Nick Lane, *Oxygen: The Molecule that made the World*, 2002, p. 155. For a chart illustrating the average minimal mutation distance in the cytochrome *c* gene between humans and various other organisms, see Donald Prothero, *Evolution: What the Fossils Say and Why it Matters*, 2007, p. 106.

that about 50% of the bases could be altered in the DNA without affecting the function of the gene. How many gene sequences could potentially generate functional protein sequences for cytochrome *c*? Mutational analysis indicates more than 2.3×10^{93} combinations are possible. What this means is that many gene sequences would yield a functional cytochrome *c* protein, but still humans and chimpanzees share an identical sequence.[213] This is strongly suggestive of common descent.[214]

The chromosome organization between humans and chimps is also highly similar, such that chimp chromosome 22 is very similar to human chromosome 21. When a further clue is revealed, this similarity is neatly explained. Francis Collins describes this amazing discovery.

> The human has 23 pairs of chromosomes, but the chimpanzee has twenty-four. The difference in the chromosome number appears to be a consequence of two ancestral chromosomes having fused together to generate human chromosome 2. That the human must be a fusion is further suggested by studying gorilla and orangutan – they each have 24 pairs of chromosomes, looking much like the chimp. Recently, with the determination of the complete human genome, it has become possible to look at the precise location where this proposed chromosomal fusion must have happened. The sequence at that location – along the long arm of chromosome 2 – is truly remarkable. Without getting into the technical details, let me say that special sequences occur at the tips of all primate chromosomes. Those sequences generally do not occur elsewhere.

---

[213] Hubert Yockey, *Information Theory and Molecular Biology*, 1992, p. 328; cited in Thomas Fowler and Daniel Kuebler, *The Evolution Controversy*, 2007, p. 183.

[214] Thomas Fowler and Daniel Kuebler, *The Evolution Controversy*, 2007, p. 183.

> But they are found right where evolution would have predicted, in the middle of our fused second chromosome. The fusion that occurred as we evolved from the apes has left its DNA imprint here. It is very difficult to understand this observation without postulating a common ancestor.[215]

Since two chromosomes from the common ancestor of all primates appear to have been fused into chromosome 2 in humans, the remaining chromosomes are staggered in relation to each other, explaining the apparent similarity in chimp chromosome 22 and human chromosome 21. The two chromosomes in apes that were fused are now referred to as chromosome 2a and chromosome 2b.

Even more suggestive of common descent is the frequent finding of *colinearity*, the relative ordering of genes and gene clusters on a chromosome. For example, in mammals, three of the four HOX clusters have a collagen and a calcium channel gene on one side and an integrin and a sodium channel gene on the other side of the cluster. The relative placement appears to be completely arbitrary as there is no functional requirement for the genes to flank the HOX cluster. Thus the gene order [Collagen] - [Ca Channel] - [HOX] - [Integrin] occurs in three places in the genome for no obvious reason other than that the genes were duplicated together during the evolutionary expansion of the genome. This phenomenon is called synteny. This gene order suggests that all mammals inherited this duplication factor from some distant ancestor.[216] Thomas Fowler gives several examples in which

---

[215] Francis Collins, *The Language of God*, 2006, p. 138.
[216] Thomas Fowler and Daniel Kuebler, *The Evolution Controversy*, 2007, p. 105.

unrelated genes are found in the same order on chromosomes of different organisms, a common finding.

> Human chromosome 9 shares synteny blocks with, among other organisms, mice and zebrafish. If one looks at human chromosome 9, one finds that it is largely a composite of regions found on mouse chromosomes 1, 4, 13 and 2. The short end of human chromosome 9 is similar to a region of mouse chromosomes 4 and 13, and the long end is similar to mouse chromosome 2.[217]

The fact that there is no known functional reason why these blocks should be ordered as they are reinforces the inference of common descent.

If common descent is true, then we would expect that the DNA would contain genes that no longer perform any meaningful function for traits that are no longer used, and that these genes should be inherited by all descendants. In contrast, if all species were specially created we would not expect to find any non-functional genes since there would be no common ancestor in which those genes were active, begging the question as to why a designer would include them.

Such "dead" genes, or pseudogenes, have been found in abundance in the genomes of eukaryotes. They may have once been useful but because of mutations they have become vestigial genes. These genes are not immediately eliminated from the DNA but simply get copied along with all the functional genes. Out of about thirty thousand genes in the human genome, over two thousand have been

---

[217] Ibid., p. 105.

identified as buried in the dead gene graveyard.[218] Evolutionary forces tend to preserve important DNA sequences, while allowing unimportant sequences to change, which accounts for why all genes with the same function have a high degree of similarity in all mammalian species. We are surprised to learn that although chickens do not have teeth, the chicken genome has genes for teeth that are never turned on, unless artificially induced.[219, 220] This observation becomes less surprising in light of the common view that birds have descended from small carnivorous dinosaurs that needed teeth for eating meat. We may require an idiom other than "hen's teeth" to identify something as "rare".

The most famous of the pseudogenes in humans is *GLO*, which when functional produced an enzyme that was used to make vitamin C. Virtually all mammals have this active gene – except for primates, fruit bats and guinea pigs, species which satisfy their requirement for vitamin C through diet. In primates and guinea pigs the gene has been disabled as a result of mutation, but since the gene was presumably not essential for survival in these species due to their ability to acquire enough vitamin C in their diet, it was passed on as a pseudogene. A closer examination of the *GLO* pseudogene yields even more evidence for common descent. In living primates GLO is more similar between close relatives than between more distant ones. For example, the pseudogene in humans and chimps is more similar than the same pseudogene in orangutans, a more distant species. Predictably the gene sequence in the guinea pig is very different from that of all primates,

---

[218] Jerry Coyne, *Why Evolution is True*, 2009, p. 67.

[219] Karl Giberson, *Saving Darwin*, 2008, p. 163.

[220] Jerry Coyne, *Why Evolution is True*, 2009, p. 66.

indicating divergence from an even earlier common ancestor. In fact the mutation that inactivated the *GLO* gene in guinea pigs happened independently at a different base pair from the mutation that caused the pseudogene in all primates. Many other pseudogenes show similar patterns, implying that pseudogenes are subject to continuous mutation through time, and thus earlier common ancestors have fewer pseudogene mutations than more recent common ancestors.[221]

A similar story can be told about our sense of smell, or lack of it. As good as our sense of smell is, we are no match for most other mammals. Most mammals such as mice have about a thousand active olfactory receptor (OR) genes, each of which codes for a receptor that recognizes a different airborne molecule. Humans have about eight hundred OR genes, but fully half of them are permanently disabled pseudogenes, and we share this condition with most other primates. How can this be explained? Probably because primates came to rely more on vision, especially color vision, and do not need to discriminate among so many odors, unneeded OR genes eventually got trashed by mutations. The example of the dolphin genome is even more striking. Dolphins have little need for smell, yet they have a large set of OR genes that resemble those of land mammals, but 80 percent of them have been inactivated. This is what one would expect from common descent if dolphins evolved from land mammals.[222]

An *intron* is a section of a gene that may display some of the same characteristics as a pseudogene. An intron consists of a non-coding DNA region within a gene. It is not translated into protein, but is removed after transcription to RNA by a process called splicing. After

---

[221] Ibid., p. 68.
[222] Ibid., p. 71.

intron splicing the RNA consists only of the exon derived sequences, which are translated into protein.

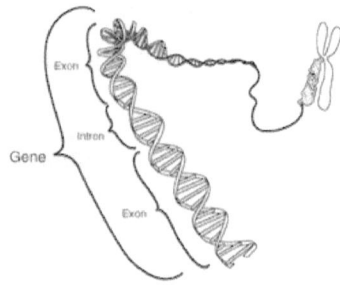

Figure 11. Sequence of nucleotides in a RNA gene showing the separation into introns and exons.

When a mutation happens in an intron, that mutation almost always has no effect on the organism because the intron is usually ignored when the body builds molecules. As with pseudogenes, if the genes in different species were similar to each other only because they share a *common design*, rather than being related by *common descent*, there would be no particular reason why the introns and their mutations in different species should show a pattern of similarity across species. On the other hand, common descent predicts that introns should show the same nested pattern of similarity that we see in pseudogenes—and that is exactly what scientists see.

Not only does the DNA molecule contain evidence for common descent, it also suggests how much time has elapsed since a critical mutation in a common ancestor occurred. Biologist Mark Ridley describes what is known as the 'molecular clock'.

> The DNA molecule seems to change during evolution at a fairly constant rate. The amount of difference between the DNA molecules of two species is therefore proportional to the time back to their common ancestor. Now imagine that we know two species had a common ancestor 10 million years ago and have accumulated ten differences in a region of their DNA. We can use this calibration point to infer the times of the common ancestors of other species pairs, once we have measured the molecular differences for them. If another pair of species has a hundred differences in that DNA region, we can infer they probably split from their common ancestor more like 100 million years ago.[223]

The molecular clock is difficult to calibrate, relies on the assumption of a constant mutation rate, and is subject to errors, especially for dates in excess of 500 million years. In spite of the erratic nature of this device, it can provide reasonable dates that can be validated by other means.

Some in the Intelligent Design movement have speculated about the possibility of the special creation of an information-rich genetic common ancestor, followed by common descent with degradation rather than common descent with modification. In *Darwin's Black Box*, Michael Behe states

> Suppose that nearly four billion years ago the designer made the first cell, already containing all of the irreducibly complex biochemical systems discussed here and many others. (One can postulate that the design for systems that were to be used later, such as blood clotting, were present but not 'turned on.' In present-day organisms plenty of genes are turned off for a while, sometimes for

---

[223] Mark Ridley, *Mendel's Demon*, 2000, p. 11.

generations, to be turned on at a later time).²²⁴

This notion has been scorned by biologists, both Christian and secular. Christian biologist Kenneth Miller of Brown University has described this scenario as "an absolutely hopeless genetic fantasy of 'pre-formed' genes waiting for the organisms that might need them to gradually appear." Biologist Sean Carroll believes this is utter nonsense that disregards the fundamentals of genetics.

> The rule of DNA is use it or lose it. The constant bombardment of mutation will erode the text of genes that are not used, as it has in icefish, yeast, humans, and virtually every other species. There is no mechanism for genes to be preserved while awaiting the need for them to arise. Rather, gene duplication, an observable process in living species, is just one means available for expanding genetic information and complexity as life evolves, and the signature of gene duplication events throughout evolution abounds in the DNA record.²²⁵

Christian biologist and theologian Denis Lamoureux has argued that the cosmos can be loaded with potentiality without being information-rich. Referring to the emerging properties of the process itself, he says

> The information to create the world is not all packed into the Big Bang. Rather, the potentiality for properties and relationships to arise exists in this initial explosive event. The evolution of a cosmos featuring the emergence of intelligent spiritual beings cries

---

[224] Michael Behe, *Darwin's Black Box*, 1996, p. 227.
[225] Sean B. Carroll, *The Making of the Fittest*, 2006, p. 244.

out for the reality of astonishing foresight, detailed planning, and incredible power.[226]

The idea of a front-loaded information-rich ancestral cell is a non-starter. A much stronger case can be made for the idea that differential reproduction has gradually added more information into the genetic structure to produce the living complexity that we see around us.

Where does new genetic information come from? Clearly the DNA contains useful information, much like the software of a computer operating system which contains useful information about the operation of the computer. Biological information is coming in (and going out) of the genome all the time.[227] Any genetic mutations that cause changes in the sequence of the amino acids in a protein represent new information. What specifies the information that is retained? Natural selection is a major factor. Sexual recombination adds new information at every conception. Information that is successfully stored in the DNA as a result of the culling of natural selection or the effect of genetic drift or any other mechanism and inherited by progeny is an addition to life's database.

Increasing complexity and increasing information content should not be taken as a built in property of common descent. In examples like the flightless birds such as ostriches, emus, penguins, and dodos, the genes coding for the token wings are better understood as losing information. Although the function of flight has been lost, in birds like the ostrich the wing stubs have been adapted to uses such as balance, a threat display, mating displays, and shading chicks in the hot sun. A

---

[226] Denis Lamoureux, *Evolutionary Creation*, 2008, p. 98.
[227] Denis Alexander, *Creation or Evolution: Do We Have to Choose?*, 2008, p. 112.

number of flightless birds like the dodo have become easy prey for predators in a changing environment and thus have gone extinct. Some cave-dwelling fish species have atrophied eyes. The cat family (lions, tigers, domestic cats) appears to have lost the function of the sweet receptor genes that are common to other mammals, making cats indifferent to sweet foods. This loss of function represents reduced information content. Complexity and information content are contingent on the environmental context, and can increase or decrease depending on the ecological requirements or influences.

Biological Baggage

A notion that argues strongly *for* common descent while simultaneously arguing *against* common design is what could be termed sub-optimal design. Biological organisms, especially the more complex forms, are rife with vestigial traits and attributes that contribute little to their original functionality but betray their ancestral roots. There is great design in nature, some of it extraordinary, but there is also enough disturbingly sub-optimal design that we should be reluctant to give direct credit to a divine Creator for it.

The notion of questionable design has already been mentioned with regard to the presence of pseudogenes in DNA, as well as the existence of unnecessary wings in flightless birds, such as ostriches. We have noted that the wing stubs are used for other purposes such as balance, but if reduced wings are the appendages used for increasing balance, why are they constructed just like wings used for flying? Darwin's answer was that "an organ rendered, during changed habits of life, useless or injurious for one purpose, might easily be modified and used for another purpose". The developmental record of horse embryos starts with the appearance of three toes, which grow at equal rates. The middle toe eventually exceeds the growth of the other two, and becomes the hoof, while the other two become "splint bones" along either side of the leg. This three-toed developmental start reflects the structure of the fossils of the feet of the 15 million year old *Merychippus* horse ancestor as seen in the fossil skeletons. It does not reflect the optimal design of a horse with a single hoof.

Many other examples of sub-optimal design exist. Whales have a pelvic structure common to all mammals, and are even sometimes born with a useless hind limb protrusion. In all mammals, the retina is 'inside out'; the nerves and blood vessels lie on the *surface* of the retina instead of behind it as is the case in many invertebrate species such as the octopus. This arrangement forces a number of complex adaptations and gives mammals a blind spot where the nerves go through the retina to get to the brain. Anyone who has had wisdom teeth removed will recognize that the human jaw no longer has the capacity to accommodate all the teeth that are programmed to emerge from the jaw. Our backs and knees are notorious for wearing out prematurely just from the normal load that they bear. At the current stage of human adaptation, these sub-optimal features can be seen as compromises in the evolutionary niche that humans occupy.

There are many more apparent poor designs in the human body. We have a single passageway for both food and air, creating the potential for food to go "down the wrong pipe" leading to choking. In the human male, testes develop initially within the abdomen, as do the gonads in the shark. Later during gestation, they migrate through the abdominal wall into the scrotum. This causes two weak points in the abdominal wall where hernias can later form. Females are not exempt from inferior reproductive design either. Their pelvises are too small to give birth easily to babies with normal sized heads. Humans have a vestigial tail, the coccyx, a triangular set of fused vertebrae attached below the pelvis. Some humans are born with useless muscles that attach to the coccyx, and some even have an atavistic tail up to a foot long that needs to be surgically removed.[228] These characteristics certainly appear to be remnants of our primate ancestry.

---

[228] Jerry Coyne, *Why Evolution is True*, 2009, p. 65.

The route of the recurrent laryngeal nerve is such that it travels from the brain to the larynx by looping around the aortic arch. This architecture is characteristic of most mammals, so in the case of the giraffe this results in about fifteen feet of extra nerve.[229] Steven Jay Gould called these throwbacks the "senseless signs of history", but if examined closely they appear to conform more closely to the Steve McGyver approach (McGyver could fix anything with a butter knife, rubber band and a roll of duct tape).

---

[229] Ibid, p. 82.

Case Study – Taking an Axe to Darwin's Tree of Life

The evidence for common descent appears overwhelming, but before presenting the assessment, let's put ourselves in the position of an ID proponent. How would an Intelligent Design proponent respond to all this evidence for a tree of life that unifies all of life? A typical approach is to poke holes in perceived weaknesses of evolutionary theory. Or would a response present empirical evidence in support of common design?

In an effort to find a strong proponent of common design, an Internet search identified a representative voice and drew my attention to http://www.discovery.org/a/10651, where lawyer Casey Luskin, a Fellow at the Discovery Institute has written A Primer on the Tree of Life. My expectation was that here would be an article that would detail strong support for common design. The first paragraph made it clear that this was instead intended to be a refutation of common descent.

Authors well-known for their support of common descent were quoted making startling statements that seemed to conflict with the basic premise of common descent. Could those authors actually have made the statements that were attributed to them? For example, there is the statement attributed to Carl Woese, a respected pioneer of evolutionary molecular systematics, who is portrayed as arguing 'that these problems extend well beyond the base of the tree of life': "Phylogenetic incongruities [conflicts] can be seen **everywhere in the universal tree, from its root to the major branchings within and among the various taxa to the makeup of the primary groupings themselves.**" [emphasis by Luskin]

I located the article from the *Proceedings of the National Academy of Sciences USA* which contained this quotation.[230] What Woese meant is that an unambiguous tree cannot be drawn for the ancestry of the three major domains of life: Archaea, Bacteria, and Eukarya, due to wholesale lateral gene transfer between their ancestors. Once the Eukarya were established, however, unambiguous Darwinian trees can be clearly deduced leading to animals, plants, and other kingdoms. The branchings are still perturbed by some lateral gene transfer but the same tree-like pattern in confirmed again and again by the analysis of more gene sequences.

Carl Woese is well known as the microbiologist and physicist who defined the Archaean domain of life as distinct from the Bacterial domain, although both are prokaryotes because they have the same cell type. Woese's paper makes it clear that the search for the root of the universal tree is being undertaken at the level of unicellular Archaea, Bacteria, and Eucarya in which a high mutation rate and lateral gene transfer prevailed. Beyond the branching of this network model of inheritance, a universal ancestor phylogenetic organismal tree emerges. The context of the final quote in Luskin's article about incongruities is limited to these "major branchings" and "primary groups". It is unfair and unreasonable to ascribe the quote to the entire Tree of Life as Luskin attempts to do. What Woese is saying is that the tree below the great ancestral branchings representing the three domains of life is only a gene tree, not an organismal tree where each node represents an identifiable life form. Luskin is being unfair not to mention this qualifying context and is making Carl Woese say something that

---

[230] Carl Woese, "The Universal Ancestor", *Proceedings of the National Academy of Sciences USA*, Vol 95:6854-9859 June 1998.

Woese did not intend to say. Luskin is guilty of either ignorance and sloppy research (perhaps he did not read the entire paper) or deliberate deception (he quoted only what was convenient for him). I do not believe Luskin is ignorant or sloppy.

Terry Gray has pointed out that Woese's "thicket of life" at the bottom of the tree does not undermine the whole molecular evolutionary enterprise.

> The evolutionary tree of eukaryotes (those derived from cytochrome c, or hemoglobin, or the eukaryotic branch of the ribosomal RNA data, etc.) is largely untouched by these interesting findings. If horizontal gene transfer is a real phenomenon, then, of course, it will complicate the determination of evolutionary relationships using sequence comparisons. But this does not undermine the whole enterprise – it just means that things are more complicated than we originally believed. But that's the way science always works! As we accumulate more data we find exceptions to our earlier more simplistic conceptions and make our models more complex to accommodate the new data. Horizontal gene transfer may indeed make it impossible to find the "universal" common ancestor, but the phenomenon itself may be telling us that our search for the "universal" common ancestor is misguided. Does this mean that evolution didn't occur? Does this now become evidence for special creation?[231]

Although Gray is responding to objections raised by Jonathan Wells, his answer applies just as well to Casey Luskin. When Luskin finds exceptions to the tree of life, those exceptions can be explained, and

---

[231] Terry Gray in Keith Miller, *Perspectives on an Evolving Creation*, 2003, p. 275.

explained in such a way that they do not invalidate the whole enterprise of common ancestry.

Luskin next enlists biologist Lynn Margulis in his support. Margulis is an eminent biologist best known for her theory of the origin of eukaryotic organelles and for her contributions to the endosymbiotic theory, now universally accepted. She showed that mitochondria and chloroplasts evolved from parasitic prokaryotes and are now actually "trapped bacteria" within eukaryotic cells. She was also president of American Scientist journal in 2006 when she wrote the opinion editorial for the journal.[232]

Here is the quote from Luskin's paper:

> Likewise, National Academy of Sciences biologist Lynn Margulis has had harsh words for the field of molecular systematics . . . In her article, "The Phylogenetic Tree Topples," she explains that "many biologists claim they know for sure that *random mutation* (purposeless chance) is the source of inherited variation that generates new species of life and that life evolved in a single-common-trunk, dichotomously branching-phylogenetic-tree pattern!" But she dissents from that view and attacks the dogmatism of evolutionary systematists, noting, "Especially dogmatic are those molecular modelers of the 'tree of life' who, ignorant of alternative topologies (such as webs), don't study ancestors."

Again, this quotation appears entirely off base. The whole point of the op-ed by Margulis was to challenge the dogmatic certainty of some molecular systematists who were ignoring confirming evidence in "animal behavior, biochemistry, comparative anatomy, ecology,

---

[232] American Scientist, Vol **94** (3) May-June 2006.

genetics, geochronology, microbiology, physiology, paleobotany, sedimentary geology, virology and zoology" and just blindly trusting comparative gene sequence data. Margulis was asking evolutionary biologists to take a more tentative, more scientific attitude towards their data. Elsewhere in the article she says "Study of long-chain molecules such as chitin, DNA, lignin, protein, yields spectacular evidence for the shared ancestry of all living matter." How could Luskin have missed this crucial point? And if he did not miss this point, why does he unfairly make Margulis out to be arguing on his behalf and against herself? Again, a very disingenuous ploy.

A third set of quotes come from an article by Antonis Rokas and Sean Carroll from an article called "Bushes in the Tree of Life".[233] Sean Carroll is a well-known author and professor of Molecular Biology, Genetics, and Medical Genetics at the University of Wisconsin-Madison, at the forefront of the field known as evolutionary developmental biology (evo-devo). Here is the Luskin quote:

> Striking admissions of troubles in reconstructing the "tree of life" also came from a paper in the journal PLOS Biology entitled, "Bushes in the Tree of Life." The authors acknowledge that "a large fraction of single genes produce phylogenies of poor quality," observing that one study "omitted 35% of single genes from their data matrix, because those genes produced phylogenies at odds with conventional wisdom." The paper suggests that "certain critical parts of the [tree of life] may be difficult to resolve, regardless of the quantity of conventional data available." The paper even contends that "[t]he recurring discovery of persistently unresolved clades

---

[233] PLOS Biology, Vol 4(11) 1899-1904 (Nov, 2006).

(bushes) should force a re-evaluation of several widely held assumptions of molecular systematics."

Unfortunately, one assumption that these evolutionary biologists aren't willing to consider changing is the assumption that neo-Darwinism and universal common ancestry are correct.

A reading of the actual paper by Rokas and Carroll gives a very different impression. Their main concern is with the "noise" factor introduced by homoplasy (similarity in species of different ancestry as the result of convergent evolution) and mutation saturation that confuses the otherwise straightforward historical branching of the genetic data:

> Can we realistically hope to resolve diversification events spanning a few or even tens of millions of years that occurred in deep time? It is widely accepted that nucleotide data are of limited use for resolving deep divergences because of mutational saturation and homoplasy. Until the recent expansion in available data, it has not been possible to fully explore what the limits of the protein record might be. Like others in the field, we also had expectations that scaling up dataset size would be sufficient to resolve interesting groups. The evidence presented here suggests that large amounts of conventional characters will not always suffice, even if analyzed by state-of-the-art methodology. Just as it would be futile to use radioisotopes with modest half lives to date ancient rocks, it appears unrealistic to expect conventional linear, homoplasy-sensitive sequences to reliably resolve series of events that transpired in a small fraction of deep time. Although we have known this from theory, we are now confronted with the actual pattern of molecular evolution.

In other words, parallel genetic changes in different organisms and multiple genetic changes in the same location distort the normal picture portrayed by the genetic mutational pattern, particularly for species divergences that occurred quickly a long time ago (in geological time). In no way do the authors question the validity of the Tree of Life or of the concept of a common ancestor. They conclude:

> Currently, phylogenetic bushes are considered experimental failures. But that is seeing the glass as half empty. A bush in which series of cladogenetic events lie crammed and unresolved within a small section of a larger tree does harbour historical information. Although it may be heresy to say so, it could be argued that knowing that strikingly different groups form a clade and that the time spans between the branching of these groups must have been very short, makes the knowledge of the branching order among groups potentially a secondary concern.

In spite of the isolated gray areas of confusion and ambiguity, these authors have no reason to change their assumption that universal common ancestry and neo-Darwinism are correct. Genes were frequently exchanged between primitive prokaryotic species through lateral gene transfer and this means that at the base there is no single tree of life, but this does not rule out the idea of a universal common ancestor. Most fundamental properties of life like the genetic code and basic metabolic pathways are shared by all of life, so even if the root of the tree is fuzzy, common ancestry is still the most likely explanation.

Three strikes! The mighty Casey has struck out! After finding that the first three references I checked had been misrepresented, there is little to conclude other than that Luskin's whole approach is one of quote mining and of misguiding his readers. A small dose of critical thinking reveals that the writing of Luskin is characteristic of the less perspicuous members of the Intelligent Design movement, and appeals strongly to the naïve and superficial, but is highly offensive to those who make the effort to delve more deeply into the intent behind the words. On this issue the Intelligent Design movement does not even speak with a unified voice. Michael Behe, a leader and a bit of a maverick in the Intelligent Design movement who holds strongly to long ages and the efficacy of natural selection writes that "It's hard to imagine how there could be stronger evidence for common ancestry of chimps and humans."[234] Considering that those in the Intelligent Design movement like Michael Behe have no issue with the idea of common descent, one wonders why Luskin would even go to the effort to make his ill-conceived argument. But then, it's not about the science. This diversity of views within the Intelligent Design movement undermines their credibility.

In view of the failure of the Intelligent Design movement to provide empirical proof of common design, we have to conclude that the concept of common design is not subject to a scientific explanation and is limited at best to what might be only a rational explanation. If common descent provides both a scientific explanation *and* a rational explanation, Occam's Razor, the principle that the simplest explanation tends to be the best one, then dictates that common descent should be chosen as a better explanation than common design.

---

[234] Michael Behe, *The Edge of Evolution*, 2007, p. 72.

Assessing the Evidence

We have examined the evidence from several different angles, including morphology, paleontology, biogeography, embryology, genetics, and the baggage of biology. In an area like morphology, we might conclude that the evidence is not strong enough to decide between common descent and common design. In all other areas, there is evidence to argue strongly for common descent.

If life on earth is *not* the result of common descent, the evidence in every area requires that the *appearance* of common descent be injected into the design of every life form. In the same unrealistic way that Young Earth Creationists argue for the *appearance* of geological age, they also must argue for the *appearance* of descent with modification. The theory of common descent, however, takes nothing away from the possibility of design itself. The distinction becomes more a difference in theories of *assembly*, but the same design. The evidence taken realistically at face value then suggests that common descent has greater explanatory weight than does common design.

When the evidence from different sets of data converges consistently on a single conclusion, it is hard not to accept the truth of the conclusion. In a 1996 message to the Pontifical Academy of Sciences, Pope John Paul III referred to evolution as "more than a hypothesis" when he stated,

> It is indeed remarkable that this theory has been progressively accepted by researchers, following a series of discoveries in various fields of knowledge. The convergence, neither sought nor fabricated, of the results of work that was conducted independently is in itself a significant argument in favor of this theory.

What makes this statement remarkable is that it addressed this convergence of evidence even prior to many of the discoveries of the last decade.

Morphological homologs have been used historically as the basis for the classification of life forms, from the hierarchical taxonomy of Linnaeus to the phylogenetic systematics of the cladists. Critics of common descent tend to confuse homology and analogy when observing similar features in different species. The case of the octopus and the human camera eye shows many anatomical similarities, but underneath the similarities are many differences. Kirschner shows how the octopus eye functions very similarly to the human eye, but that it arrives at that function via a different developmental route.

> The [octopus] eye derives from different tissues by different developmental means. Although both structures use the same pigment (rhodopsin) for photoreception, and both send electrical signals to the brain, we now know that the intervening circuitry is completely different. Nonetheless, both have drawn on various cellular and developmental processes and components of the toolbox common to bilateral animals, using different tools in a different order. That the phototransduction circuits are completely different (involving components that are different but common to both organisms) is a testimonial to the power of conserved processes – they can be organized by different means to a similar end. In convergence, similar outcomes are evolved in different ways, making use of exploratory processes, modularity, flexibility and weak linkage. Anatomical convergence at the level of these

processes is no different than anatomical diversification."[235]

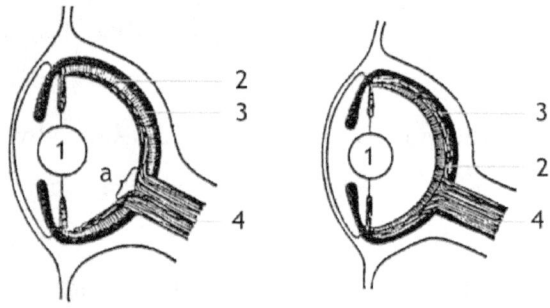

Figure 12. Human (left) and octopus (right) analogous eye structures, with lens (1), photoreceptors (2), retina (3), and optic nerve (4).

Octopus eyes, rather than being homologous to human camera eyes, are analogous to them. They result from similar environmental and development pressures but do not necessarily derive from a common ancestor. Thus we see that the study of morphology has become much more sophisticated than it was in Darwin's day, to the extent that it is now supported by further knowledge in physiology and molecular biology. Kirschner illustrates how analogous features like the octopus eye and human eye have travelled different pathways to result in the same solution, and homologous features like the vertebrate limb that have travelled similar pathways to result in different solutions.

> The deeper we probe into the development, physiology, and anatomy of the octopus eye, the more we see how completely different it is from the vertebrate eye. But as we probe each vertebrate limb, the opposite happens. On the deepest molecular

---

[235] Marc Kirschner and John Gerhart, *The Plausibility of Life*, 2005, p. 240.

level of selector genes and signaling pathways in their development, the limbs of all vertebrates are strikingly similar. They form at exactly the same position relative to the segmented muscle blocks. The pectoral fins of fish use the same selector genes as the forelimbs of the mouse, whereas the pelvic fins use a different factor, the same as the hindlimbs. The detailed patterning of the front-to-back selector genes is the same in all limbs.[236]

If it can be shown that homologies do exist and appear to arise from common ancestors, then the question arises as to where these features originate. Kirschner asks,

> Where do the differences arise in the limbs of bats, porpoises, horses, and humans? As one might expect from facilitated variation, they come from the timing of, and amounts of, the secreted factors and selector genes affecting the growth of the various limb bones. The greatest differences are in the digits, reflecting their diversity. If we ask about the irreducible complexity of the limb, we see that it has avoided that problem in its evolution by the highly adaptive exploratory systems of the muscle, vascular system, and nerves – all of which migrate, proliferate, and make functional connections relative to the skeletal elements. The homology of limbs was one of the triumphs of evolutionary biology in the nineteenth century; they are more deeply understood than any other anatomical structure, and the modern molecular evidence for homology, its development, and its evolution, is unassailable.[237]

---

[236] Marc Kirschner and John Gerhart, *The Plausibility of Life*, 2005, p. 270.
[237] Ibid., p. 270.

In other words, the basic body plan, which is dictated by the HOX type genes and which appears in the final anatomy of each related species in the form of homologous structures, is modified during development to support the peculiar needs of each species. Each species has a unique set of morphogenetic genes that regulate and tailor the expression of the developmental genes. The developmental genes cooperate with the morphogenetic genes to produce the refining features of each species. For example, even though the genome of the chicken and the mouse both support the development of teeth, the morphogenetic genes of the chicken suppress this growth. Homologous features strongly suggest common descent with modifications. Analogous features strongly suggest common descent through convergent evolution.

In paleontology, the frequent recent discovery of many transitional fossils fills in many of the gaps that troubled Darwin.

Designing a horse

The speciation, diversification, adaptations, rates of change, trends and extinctions over 55 million years in the evolution of horses as seen in their fossil record is a classic example of common descent with modification. Could the same patterns be explained by common design? The pattern of horse speciation tracks closely the changes in vegetation that took place during their evolution. The link between climate, food source and species succession is exactly what one would expect to find on the assumption that they drive common descent with modification.[238] Of course, an intentional designer could make each of the three dozen species in the fossil record separately and then watch

---

[238] Kenneth Miller, *Only a Theory*, 2008, p. 50.

nearly all of them go extinct, acting more like a "serial creator" than a designer. "He brings into being new species again and again, inexplicably fashioning each one so that it bears a striking resemblance to a species just lost to extinction. In other words, intelligent design is actually a hypothesis of progressive creationism."[239] Kenneth Miller concludes that if common design theory is taken seriously, it is just another form of creationism that keeps the designer / creator working over billions of years creating each new species, biological novelty, gene, pathway and biochemical machine from scratch. This would suggest that each new design is in fact a failed design.

Designing a human

The following chart shows six different hominid fossil skulls and the verdict of a number of proponents of the common design theory as to whether they belonged to apes or humans. A design proponent wants a clear demarcation between a non-human and a human species, and as we expect, each publication clearly identifies each skull as either ape or human. What is instructive is that there is such a disparity between the publications! If there is such a wide gap separating humans and apes, deciding on which side of the gap individual fossils lie should be trivially easy. Clearly that is not the case. Not a single one design proponent agrees with another. Which one is correct?

---

[239] Ibid., p. 52.

Specimen	Cuozzo (1998)	Gish (1985)	Mehlert (1996)	Bowden (1981) Menton (1988) Taylor (1992) Gish (1979)	Baker (1976) Taylor and Van Bebber (1995)	Taylor (1996) Lubenow (1992)	Line (2005)
ER 1813 (510 cc)	Ape	Ape	Ape	Ape	Ape	Ape	Human ??[2]
Java (940 cc)	Ape	Ape	Human	Ape	Ape	Human	Human
Peking (915-1225 cc)	Ape	Ape	Human	Ape	Human	Human	Human
ER 1470 (750 cc)	Ape	Ape	Ape	Human	Human	Human[1]	Human ??[2]
ER 3733 (850 cc)	Ape	Human	Human	Human	Human	Human	Human
WT 15000 (880 cc)	Ape	Human	Human	Human	Human	Human	Human

Figure 13. **Six different hominid fossil skulls, and the differing opinions of eight different creationist publications.**

We really do not know where the divide between apes and humans lies, and that is precisely the point. As Kenneth Miller concludes, "What better proof could one offer of the transitional nature of the human fossil record than the profound lack of agreement of antievolutionists as to how to classify these fossils? Ironically, validation of our common ancestry with other primates comes directly from those who are most critical of the idea."[240] Again, common

---

[240] Kenneth Miller, *Only a Theory*, 2008, p. 95.

descent is strongly validated in its power to explain the ancestry pattern.

In our earlier discussion of biogeography, we noted that the observed geographic distribution of plants and animals can best be explained by a naturalistic radiation of organisms via common descent through natural selection. Thus few mammals are expected or observed on the Hawaiian or Galapagos islands. Also the organisms that are endemic to those islands are those most similar to the inhabitants of the nearest continent. Their ancestors likely came from those continents and then underwent speciation on the islands, evolving into their different and diverse forms. The nature of common descent with modification provides the best explanation for the existence and geographical location of such species.

The existence of ring species, as discussed earlier, provides strong evidence for the idea that many small changes can eventually accumulate into large differences between distinct species. Some critics of evolutionary theory think that evolution can only cause limited change within a species and cannot lead to the evolution of new species. The ring species data show that they are wrong, and even show that complete geographical isolation is not necessary to produce new species.

Another argument for common descent is that it provides the best explanation for the observed pattern of life forms in their related ecological zone. If a Creator specially created species to fill each ecological niche, it is difficult to find a reason for the particular pattern that developed. But if a Creator used common descent and evolutionary processes to fill those ecological niches, the pattern makes sense.[241]

A Star is Born

Even though the Bible tells us that humans are unique because they bear the image of God, their biological development is similar to the rest of the animal kingdom and can be traced from beginning to end as a continuous natural process. Speaking about the embryos of the different life forms, Kenneth Miller says:

> Each of these embryos possesses the same developmental tool kit, revealing both their common ancestry and a similarity of form and function produced by the workings of the evolutionary process. Today the vertebrate embryo not only argues for the reality of evolution, it also helps to show us in detail how that process works.[242]

According to Sean Carroll, evolutionary development blurs the distinction between the two types of changes referred to as microevolution and macroevolution.

> The continuity of the tool kit and the continuity of structures throughout this vast time illustrate that we need not invoke rare or special mechanisms to explain large-scale change. The extrapolation from small-scale variation to large-scale evolution is well justified. In evolutionary parlance, Evo Devo reveals that

---

[241] Deborah Haarsma and Loren Haarsma, *Origins: A Reformed Look at Creation, Design, and Evolution*, 2007, p. 166.

[242] Kenneth Miller, *Only a Theory*, 2008, p. 131.

macroevolution is the product of microevolution writ large.[243]

This is not what the Intelligent Design movement wants to hear. If scientists already have the capacity to account for the living world, the *scientific* case for intelligent design has failed. Within the scientific context Kenneth Miller offers, "The wonder of life is that the capacity for changing its own recipe is built right into it."[244]

In addressing the question of whether HOX genes are an indicator of common descent or common design, Michael Ruse suggests:

> It is clear that evolution is a tremendous re-user of what is already available, putting the same things to work in all sorts of different organisms. If it functions for one, then let's use it for others. We find also at the molecular level that we get many instances of what in the nineteenth century was known as "serial homology", where the same part (for example, a vertebra) is used again and again in the same organism. Time and again at the molecular level, instead of inventing a new gene or a new process or a new structure, existing genes or processes or structures are duplicated or triplicated or more, and then put to use in the same or slightly different ways.[245]

Those who find comfort in the idea that common descent does not explain what they call "macroevolution" will be disappointed with the relatively recent findings from genetics and microbiology. Terry Gray reports that he continues to be amazed at skeptics who point to the

---

[243] Sean B. Carroll, *Endless Forms Most Beautiful*, 2005, p. 291.

[244] Kenneth Miller, *Only a Theory*, 2008, p. 133.

[245] Michael Ruse, *Charles Darwin*, 2008, p. 155.

Cambrian explosion and the "sudden" appearance of animal phyla and who seem to ignore the relationships indicated by the molecular and genetic data.[246] He points out that although the genetic code displays a deep unity through all life forms, the historical events of chromosomal alterations have resulted in recognizably distinct but related species.

> The genetic similarity suggests common ancestry, although special creationists will appeal to common design. But, why the differences if there is common design? The differences in light of the unity are what make the evolutionary argument so compelling. The rearrangements are readily understood as historical events superimposed upon the functional genome. Due to the nature of sexual reproduction at the cellular level, rearrangements will wreak havoc on chromosome alignment and recombination events, so such historical events are not without significance. The evolution envisioned here is macroevolutionary in nature. We are determining relationships between major orders of mammals via this mode of analysis.[247]

The anomalies and intermediate stages in human embryology and the conserved core processes identified by the evolutionary development biologists like Sean Carroll and Marc Kirschner strongly suggest that humans share a history with all of life on earth.

---

[246] Terry Gray in Keith Miller, *Perspectives on an Evolving Creation*, 2003, p. 281.
[247] Ibid., p. 283.

It's in the genes

As noted earlier, the genomes of widely different life forms share similar genetic patterns. The genetic patterns of more closely related species show more similarity than the more distantly related ones. Opponents of common descent might argue that these genetic similarities reflect not common ancestry, but similar functionality. After all, if eagles, hummingbirds, robins and meadowlarks all fly, one would expect that the genetic program to produce the required similar flight-capable body structure would be similar.

This *common function* or *common design* theory runs into a number of problems. It fails to explain why flightless birds such as ostriches and emus still have genetic patterns related to flight. The rational conclusion of common descent is that these birds lost their flight capability when it was no longer required for them, and their DNA simply retained the genetic structure that once provided this capability. Common design theory fails to explain why bats do not have the genetic support for bird-like wings, yet their genetic pattern is much more similar to rats than to that of birds.

An even greater problem for the common design theory is the existence of *pseudogenes*, genes that were presumably functional but became disabled due to mutations. Ordinarily one would expect genetic mutations that stop a gene from functioning to harm the organism, but when the gene is not essential for survival and reproduction, that mutated gene becomes DNA baggage and is known as a *pseudogene*. The most frequently cited case is a gene for vitamin C synthesis which is enabled in most mammals but disabled in primates. This makes sense if primates share a common ancestor with other mammals. The vitamin C synthesis gene in this common ancestor was disabled by a mutation that proved not to be fatal. Based on the common design theory, there is no reason for this pseudogene or any others to exist.

Jerry Coyne raises a number of questions about why we should see these patterns in the genome if all species were specially created.

> Why would a creator put a pathway for making vitamin C in all these species, and then inactivate it? Wouldn't it be easier simply to omit the whole pathway from the beginning? Why would the same inactivating mutation be present in all primates, and a different one in guinea pigs? Why would the sequences of the dead gene exactly mirror the pattern of resemblance predicted from the known ancestry of these species? And why do humans have thousands of pseudogenes in the first place?[248]

These rhetorical questions are meant to challenge us to question whether God the Creator would ask us to disbelieve something that nature is telling us. If nature is an expression of God's creative power, would God deliberately mislead us about what nature reveals to us? If the evidence of science overwhelmingly supports common ancestry, would God's revealed Word tell us otherwise? If all the evidence points to a universe that is billions of years old, would God ask us to believe the world was created only six to ten thousand years ago? Or are we simply misunderstanding what the Bible's message is all about?

With respect to the human sense of smell, Coyne answers his own question.

---

[248] Jerry Coyne, *Why Evolution is True*, 2009, p. 69.

> If you look at the sequences of human olfactory receptor (OR) genes, both active and inactive, they are most similar to those of other primates, less similar to those of "primitive" mammals like the platypus, and less similar yet to the OR genes of distant relatives like reptiles. Why should dead genes show such a relationship, if not for evolution? And the fact that we harbor so many inactive genes is even more evidence for evolution: we carry this genetic baggage because it was needed in our distant ancestors who relied for survival on a keen sense of smell.[249]

Francis Collins is unconvinced about the appeal to common design as an explanation for common genetic function.

> Some might argue that these are actually functional elements placed there by the Creator for a good reason, and our discounting of them as "junk DNA" just betrays our current level of ignorance. And indeed, some small fraction of them may play important regulatory roles. But certain examples severely strain the credulity of that explanation. The process of transposition often damages the jumping gene. There are AREs (ancient repetitive elements) throughout the human and mouse genomes that were truncated when they landed, removing any possibility of their functioning. In many instances, one can identify a decapitated and utterly defunct ARE in parallel positions in the human and the mouse genome.[250]

And so, on the basis of the preceding evidence, the strongest explanation of life's genetic program appears to be common descent.

---

[249] Jerry Coyne, *Why Evolution is True*, 2009, p. 71.
[250] Francis Collins, *The Language of God*, 2006, p. 136.

Life's Baggage

In his book *Darwin's Black Box*, Michael Behe acknowledges that suboptimal features of design exist and claims that "features that strike us as odd in a design might have been placed there by the Designer for a reason – for artistic reasons, for variety, to show off, for some as-yet-undetectable practical purpose, or for some unguessable reason – or they might not."[251] Based on the evidence, common design proponents likely do not want to pass off bad design features as some whimsical incompetence. These features appear as though they have evolved, and it seems unlikely that a Creator would have made them appear that way when in fact they had not resulted from common descent. However, even Behe concedes that common descent is the best explanation for our physical existence.

> In the past hundred years science has advanced enormously; what do the results of modern science show? In brief, the evidence for common descent seems compelling. The results of modern DNA sequencing experiments, undreamed of by nineteenth-century scientists like Charles Darwin, show that some distantly related organisms share apparently arbitrary features of their genes that seem to have no explanation other than that they were inherited from a distant common ancestor. Second, there's also great evidence that random mutation paired with natural selection can modify life in important ways. Third, however, there is strong evidence that random mutation is extremely limited.[252]

---

[251] Michael Behe, *Darwin's Black Box*, 1996, p. 223.
[252] Ibid., p. 3.

He goes on to describe in great detail why he comes to those conclusions, using evidence from hemoglobin and the effect of sickle cell anemia on malaria. For example,

> When two lineages share what appears to be an arbitrary genetic accident, the case for common descent becomes compelling, just as the case for plagiarism becomes overpowering when one writer makes the same unusual misspellings of another, within a copy of the same words. That sort of evidence is seen in the genomes of humans and chimpanzees. For example, both humans and chimps have a broken copy of a gene that in other mammals helps make vitamin C. As a result, neither humans nor chimps make their own vitamin C. If an ancestor of the two species originally sustained the mutation and then passed it to both descendant species, that would neatly explain the situation.[253]

"Poor design" is consistent with the predictions of common descent with modification by means of natural selection. This theory predicts that features that were first evolved for certain uses were then reused or co-opted for different uses, or abandoned altogether; and the sub-optimal state is due to the historical contingencies of natural selection preserving only what works best for a given environment. The hereditary mechanism is an adaptive process and is unable to eliminate completely the particular vestiges of the evolutionary process. Natural selection has the effect of preserving the best adaptations, but this is always relative to the existing genotype (including its historical baggage) and the local environment. The effect of these parameters is

---

[253] Ibid., p. 71.

referred to as a fitness landscape[254] and can be visualized as local peaks of adaptation. In terms of a fitness landscape, natural selection always pushes "up the hill", and a species cannot normally get from a lower peak to a higher peak without first going through a valley, and the peak at which it finds itself is often not the highest. The presence of putative poor design only makes sense if the observed unfavourable features evolved from adaptive features of earlier ancestors. It seems that we are constrained by our evolutionary history.

Designing Life

Much evidence, both factual and inferred, has been provided to support the likelihood of common descent through naturalistic mechanisms. Evidence cited *can* be explained by putting a supernatural spin on the science if one believes that the common architecture is similar in closely related species because the designer struck upon an exceedingly robust plan and reused it again and again. However, if a naturalistic explanation of the similarities is available, little room is left for special creation. Invoking special creation only creates a Godly gap that has the potential of later being filled in with further scientific evidence, thereby discrediting God. Even the origin of life, although not strictly part of evolution or common descent, should not be held in reserve as a unique act of supernatural intervention.

The evidence we have examined suggests that there is an intimate relationship between design and descent, and that design is not limited to the form of every species. This requires that we move beyond the notion that a single-shot creative effort was required to create every

---

[254] For a full treatment on this topic see Richard Dawkins, *Climbing Mount Improbable*, 1996.

single species individually. Design and descent then are intimately intertwined. This conception of design is not evident as proof in nature, but is pervasive and persuasive. Even Richard Dawkins refers to the unmistakable "appearance of design", although he characteristically attributes it all to natural causes. But this is a design that has a theological understanding that creation has a divine purpose and plan – that it is intelligently and intentionally conceived. From a Christian perspective, although somewhat overstated, Kenneth Miller also recognizes design, calling it "deep and profound":

> Evolution really does tell us something deep and profound about the world in which we live – something that Darwin glimpsed but that is much more obvious today. As it turns out, there really is a design to life, but it's not the clumsy, interventionist one in which life is an artificial injection into nature, a contradiction of its physical laws. Rather, it is a design in which life emerges from the laws of the universe around us. That conclusion is unavoidable, robust and scientific. The elegant universe is a universe of life. And the name of the grand design of life is evolution.[255]

Frederick Temple, Archbishop of Canterbury who died in 1902, attributed the deep and profound mystery of design to the subtle and powerful creativity and mastery of a God who creates a nature to evolve itself. He states "God doesn't just make the world, he does something even more wonderful, He makes the world make itself." The creation of a "life factory" is a concept that is much more profound, shows much more intelligent design, and is more intellectually and theologically satisfying than the repeated incremental episodic miraculous formation of every species of life. Kenneth Miller alludes to the fine-tuning required to allow this incredible design to be realized:

> However one accounts for the nature of our universe, however one explains the perfection of its recipe of constants, one fact remains: We live in a universe where the conditions that make life possible are built into the material fabric of existence. The ways in which matter and energy behave in our world are not only consistent with life, but are absolutely necessary for it. In effect the architecture of our universe, from the structure of a grain of sand to the unimaginable expanses of galaxies, is a blueprint for life – maybe, even, for human life.[256]

Even an atheist like Eugenie Scott, executive director of the National Center for Science Education (NCSE) since 1987, allows for the action of an all-powerful God but outside the reach of science to prove: "Any action of an omnipotent Creator is compatible with any and all scientific explanations of the natural world. The methods of science cannot choose among the possible actions of an omnipotent Creator."[257] Owen Gingerich also weighs in on the relationship between science and nature, and how we perceive design:

> In reflecting on the question of design, I have attempted to delineate a subtle place for it in the world of science. Intimations of design can offer persuasion regarding the role of divine creativity in the universe, but never proof. Science remains a neutral way of

---

[255] Kenneth Miller, *Only a Theory*, 2008, p.134.
[256] Ibid., p.122.

explaining things, not anti-God or atheistic.[258]

Although the evidence does not provide a "scientific explanation" for design, this does not negate design as a "rationale explanation" for nature.[259] Owen Gingerich explains that the reductionism that sees life as only a collection of elementary components does not take into account the built-in properties that fuel the emergent properties when these components form relationships:

> "Design" should not necessarily be taken to mean the detailed working out of a preordained pattern. A combination of contingency and natural selection can produce organisms exquisitely attuned to their environment, true marvels that stagger our imaginations. But contingency and natural selection do not create the extraordinary physical and chemical conditions – the solubilities, the diffusion coefficients, the bonding strengths, and so on – that permit the existence of such marvels. It is like having a giant and very complex Lego set supplied without a blueprint. There may be no architect with a plan for the final product, but there is the designer of the set of little interlocking parts. And the existence of the set itself cries out for something to be built with it.[260]

He leaves no doubt that in his mind there *is* a grand architect who has a definite plan in mind.

---

[257] Eugenie Scott, *Evolution vs. Creationism*, 2005, p. 19-20.
[258] Owen Gingerich, *God's Universe*, 2006, p. 78.
[259] See Thomas Fowler and Daniel Kuebler, *The Evolution Controversy*, 2007, p. 124-125.
[260] Owen Gingerich, *God's Universe*, 2006, p. 37.

> I am personally persuaded that a superintelligent Creator exists beyond and within the cosmos, and that the rich context of congeniality shown by our universe, permitting and encouraging the existence of self-conscious life, is part of the Creator's design and purpose.[261]

Gingerich sees evidence of design even in the properties and contingencies built into the elemental components:

> We could ask whether God designed the universe in the first place to make possible the catalysts and unknown pathways that enable the formation of life. I mentioned the incredible odds against the chance formation of a protein molecule. For science to overcome the odds, it is necessary for us to postulate the existence of those pathways, and it is of course precisely the challenge of science to discover such pathways. But is not the existence of such pathways also evidence of design? And are they not inevitable? These are questions that materialists do not want to hear.[262]

Common descent provides a compelling answer to the question of the continuity of all of natural life. Although this is an entirely naturalistic explanation, it does not preclude the notion that God as Creator caused the earth to be formed with the intentional capability of harnessing common descent. Instead of the static creation of each species, however that might come about, the dynamic emergence of all life including vulnerable creatures that themselves become creative through common descent reflects the exquisite creativity of the designer.

---

[261] Ibid., p. 39.
[262] Ibid., p. 71.

Common descent gives more dignity, not less, to the created beings. As co-creators, we bear the image of the Creator, and as we exercise our creativity, we can say with the Creator, "It is good."

Significantly, supernatural results may be achieved through what seem like "natural" processes. God as Sustainer continues to uphold the natural laws that cause life to evolve. God as Redeemer, Saviour and Friend continues to work subtly and miraculously in our lives so that His glory may be known.

This is what the Lord says: "Let not the wise man boast of his wisdom or the strong man boast of his strength or the rich man boast of his riches, but let him who boasts boast about this: that he understands and knows me, that I am the Lord, who exercises kindness, justice and righteousness on earth, for in these I delight," declares the Lord.

- Jeremiah 9:23

References and Further Reading

Alexander, Denis, *Rebuilding the Matrix: Science and Faith in the 21st Century*, 2001

Alexander, Denis, *Evolution or Creation? Do We Have to Choose*, 2008

Alexander, Denis & Numbers, Ronald, *Biology and Ideology: From Descartes to Dawkins*, 2010

Alters, Brian J., Alters, Sandra M., *Defending Evolution: A guide to the creation/evolution controversy*, 2001

Avise, John, 2010, *Inside the Human Genome: A Case for Non-Intelligent Design*

Barbour, Ian G., *When Science Meets Religion: Enemies, Strangers or Partners?*, 2000

Barr, Stephen M., *Modern Physics and Ancient Faith*, 2006

Barrow, John D., Tipler, Frank J., *The Left Hand of Creation: The Origin and Evolution of the Expanding Universe*, 1983

Barrow, John D., Tipler, Frank J., *The Anthropic Cosmological Principle*, 1986

Barrow, John D., *The Origin of the Universe*, 1994

Barrow, John D., *The Artful Universe*, 1995

Behe, Michael J., *Darwin's Black Box: The Biochemical Challenge to Evolution*, 1996

Behe, Michael J., *The Edge of Evolution: The Search for the Limits of Darwinism*, 2007

Berlinski, David, *Newton's Gift: How Sir Isaac Newton Unlocked the System of the World*, 2000

Berlinski, David, *The Devil's Delusion: Atheism and its Scientific Pretensions*, 2009

Bowler, Peter J., *Monkey Trials & Gorilla Sermons: Evolution and Christianity from Darwin to Intelligent Design*, 2007

Bray, Dennis, *Wetware: A Computer in Every Cell*, 2009

Bryson, Bill, *A Short History of Nearly Everything*, 2003

Cairns-Smith, A. G., *Seven Clues to the Origin of Life*, 1985

Carroll, Sean B., *Endless Forms Most Beautiful: The New Science of Evo Devo*, 2005

Carroll, Sean B., *The Making of the Fittest: DNA and the Ultimate Forensic Record of Evolution*, 2006

Carroll, Sean B., 2009, *Remarkable Creatures: Epic Adventures in the Search for the Origins of Species*

Colling, Richard G., *Random Designer*, 2004

Collins, C. John, *Science & Faith: Friends or Foes?*, 2003
Collins, Francis, *The Language of God: A Scientist Presents Evidence for Belief*, 2006
Covey, Stephen, *Seven Habits of Highly Effective* People, 1989
Coyne, Jerry A., *Why Evolution is True*, 2009
Crick, Francis, *Life Itself: Its Origin and Nature*, 1981
Dalrymple, G. Brent, *The Age of the Earth*, 1991
Davies, Paul, *The Accidental Universe*, 1982
Davies, Paul, *God and the New Physics*, 1983
Davies, Paul, *The Mind of God*, 1992
Davies, Paul, *The Cosmic Jackpot: Why Our Universe is Just Right for Life*, 2007
Dawkins, Richard, *The Selfish Gene*, 1976
Dawkins, Richard, *The Blind Watchmaker*, 1986
Dawkins, Richard, *Climbing Mount Improbable*, 1996
Dawkins, Richard, *The Ancestor's Tale*, 2004
de Duve, Christian, *Vital Dust: The Origin and Evolution of Life on Earth*, 1995
Dembski, William, *Mere Creation: Science, Faith & Intelligent Design*, 1995
Dembski, William, *Intelligent Design: The Bridge Between Science and Theology*, 1999
Dembski, William, *Uncommon Dissent*, 2004
Dembski, William, *Darwin's Nemesis: Phillip Johnson and the Intelligent Design Movement*, 2006
Dembski, William and McDowell, Sean, *Understanding Intelligent Design*, 2008
Dennett, Daniel C., *Darwin's Dangerous Idea*, 1995
Dennett, Daniel C., *Breaking the Spell*, 2006
Denton, Michael, *Evolution: A Theory in Crisis: New Developments in Science are Challenging Orthodox Darwinism*, 1985
Diamond, Jared, *The Third Chimpanzee: The Evolution and Future of the Human Animal*, 1992
Diamond, Jared, *Guns, Germs, and Steel: The Fates of Human Societies*, 1997
Dobzhansky, Theodosius, *Mankind Evolving*, 1962
Dyson, Freeman, *Disturbing the Universe*, 1979
Falk, Darrel R., *Coming to Peace with Science:Bridging the Worlds Between Faith and Biology*, 2004
Fairbanks, Daniel, *Relics of Eden: The Powerful Evidence of Evolution in Human DNA*, 2007

Ferris, Timothy, *The Red Limit: The Search for the Edge of the Universe*, 1983
Ferris, Timothy, *Coming of Age in the Milky Way*, 1988
Filler, Dr. Aaron G., *The Upright Ape: A New Origin of the Species*, 2007
Finocchiaro, Maurice A., *The Galileo Affair: A Documentary History*, 1989
Fowler, Thomas B., Kuebler, Daniel, *The Evolution Controversy*, 2007
Giberson, Karl, W., *Oracles of Science: Celebrity Scientists versus God and Religion*, 2007
Giberson, Karl W., *Saving Darwin: How to be a Christian and Believe in Evolution*, 2008
Gingerich, Owen, *God's Universe*, 2006
Godfrey, Stephen J. and Smith, Christopher R., *Paradigms on Pilgrimage: Creationism, Paleontology, and Biblical Interpretation*, 2005
Gonzales, Guillermo and Richards, Jay, *The Privileged Planet: How our Place in the Cosmos is Designed for Discovery*, 2004
Goodsell, David, *The Machinery of Life*, 2009
Goodwin, Brian, *How the Leopard Changed Its Spots: The Evolution of Complexity*, 1994
Gould, Stephen Jay, *The Panda's Thumb*, 1980
Gould, Stephen Jay, *Ever Since Darwin: Reflections in Natural History*, 1973
Gould, Stephen Jay, *Wonderful Life: The Burgess Shale and the Nature of History*, 1989
Gould, Stephen Jay, *Rocks of Ages: Science and Religion in the Fullness of Life*, 1999
Gould, Stephen Jay, *I Have Landed: The End of a Beginning in Natural History*, 2003
Greene, Brian, *The Elegant Universe*, 2003
Greene, Brian, *The Fabric of the Universe*, 2004
Gribbin, John, 1985, *In Search of the Double Helix*
Haarsma, Deborah and Haarsma, Loren, *Origins: A Reformed Look at Creation, Design and Evolution*, 2007
Harris, Sam, *The End of Faith: Religion, Terror, and the Future of Reason*, 2004
Harrison, Ed, *Cosmology*, 2000
Haught, John F., *God After Darwin: A Theology of Evolution*, 2000
Haught, John F., *Is Nature Enough? : Meaning and Truth in the Age of Science*, 2006

Haught, John F., *Christianity and Science: Toward a Theology of Nature*, 2007
Hawking, Stephen, *A Brief History of Time*, 1992
Hazen, Robert M., *Genesis: The Scientific Quest for Life's Origin*, 2005
Heeren, Fred, *Show me God: What the Message from Space is Telling Us About God*, 1998
Hoyle, Fred, *Frontiers of Astronomy*, 1955
Hoyle, Fred, *Highlights of Astronomy*, 1975
Humes, Edward, *Monkey Girl: Evolution, Education, Religion, and the Battle for America's Soul*, 2007
Hunter, Cornelius, *Darwin's Proof: The Triumph of Religion over Science*, 2003
Jastrow, Robert, *God and the Astronomers*, 1978
Jennings, William H., *Storms Over Genesis: Biblical Battleground in America's Wars of Religion*, 2007
Johnson, Phillip E., *Darwin on Trial*, 1991
Johnson, Phillip E., Lamoureaux, Denis, *Darwinism Defeated? The Johnson-Lamoureux Debate on Biological Origins*, 1999
Jones, Steve, *Darwin's Ghost*, 1999
Judson, Horace Freeland, *The Eighth Day of Creation: The Makers of the Revolution in Biology*, 1979
Keller, Timothy, *The Reason for God: Belief in an Age of Skepticism*, 2008
Kirschner, Marc W. and Gerhart, John C., *The Plausibility of Life: Resolving Darwin's Dilemma*, 2005
Kuhn, Thomas S., *The Structure of Scientific Revolutions*, 1996
Lamoureux, Denis, *Evolutionary Creation: A Christian Approach to Evolution*, 2008
Lane, Nick, *Oxygen: The Molecule that made the World*, 2002
Lane, Nick, *Power, Sex, Suicide: Mitochondria and the Meaning of Life*, 2005
Lane, Nick, *Life Ascending: The Ten Great Inventions of Evolution*, 2009
Larson, Edward J., *Trial and Error: The American Controvery over Creation and Evolution*, 1985
Larson, Edward J., *Summer for the Gods: The Scopes Trial and America's Continuing Debate Over Science and Religion*, 1997
Larson, Edward J., *Evolution: The Remarkable History of a Scientific Theory*, 2004
Lennox, John C., *God's Undertaker: Has Science Buried God*, 2009
Lewis, C.S., *God in the Dock*, 1970

Lloyd, Seth, *Programming the Universe*, 2007
Martin, Joel, *The Prism and the Rainbow*, 2010
Mayr, Ernst, *What Evolution Is*, 2001
McGrath, Alister, *The Science of God*, 2004
McGrath, Alister, *Dawkins' God: Genes, Memes, and the Meaning of Life*, 2005
McGrath, Alister, *The Dawkins Delusion? : Atheist Fundamentalism and the Denial of the Divine*, 2007
McLaren, Brian, *The Story We Find Ourselves In: Further Adventures of a New Kind of Christian*, 2004
Meyer, Stephen, *Signature in the Cell: DNA and the Evidence for Intelligent Design*, 2009
Miller, Keith, *Perspectives on an Evolving Creation*, 2003
Miller, Kenneth R., *Finding Darwin's God: A Scientist's Search for Common Ground Between God and Evolution*, 1999
Miller, Kenneth R., *Only a Theory: Evolution and the Battle for America's Soul*, 2008
Mills, David, *Atheist Universe: The Thinking Person's Answer to Christian Fundamentalism*, 2006
Monod, Jacques, *Chance and Necessity*, 1970
Moreland, J.P., *Kingdom Triangle: Recover the Christian Mind, Renovate the Soul, Restore the Spirit's Power*, 2007
Morowitz, Harold J., *The Emergence of Everything: How the World Became Complex*, 2002
Morris, Henry and Whitcomb, John, *The Genesis Flood: The Biblical Record and its Scientific Implications*, 1961
Morris, Simon Conway, *The Crucible of Creation: The Burgess Shale and the Rise of Animals*, 1995
Morris, Simon Conway, *Life's Solution: Inevitable Humans in a Lonely Universe*, 2003
Noll, Mark, *The Scandal of the Evangelical Mind*, 1994
Numbers, Ronald L., *The Creationists: From Scientific Creationism to Intelligent Design*, 1992
O'Leary, Denyse, *Faith@Science: Why Science Needs Faith in the Twenty-First Century*, 2001
O'Leary, Denyse, *By Design or by Chance?: The Growing Controversy on the Origins of Life in the Universe*, 2004
Pais, Abraham, *'Subtle is the Lord': The Science and the Life of Albert Einstein*, 1982
Patterson, Colin, *Evolution*, 1978
Perakh, Mark, *Unintelligent* Design, 2004

Peters, Ted and Hewlett, Martinez, *Evolution from Creation to New Creation: Conflict, Conversion, and Convergence*, 2003
Peters, Ted and Hewlett, Martinez, *Can You Believe in God and Evolution? A Guide for the Perplexed*, 2006
Plantinga, Alvin, *Faith and Rationality: Reason and Belief in God*, 1983
Polkinghorne, John, *The Faith of a Physicist*, 1996
Polkinghorne, John, *Quantum Physics and Theology*, 2007
Poythress, Vern, 2006, *Redeeming Science*
Prothero, Donald, 2007, *Evolution: What the Fossils Say and Why it Matters*
Raymo, Chet, *Skeptics and True Believers: The Exhilarating Connection Between Science and Religion*, 1998
Rees, Martin, *Just Six Numbers: The Deep Forces that Shape the Universe*, 1999
Ridley, Mark, *Mendel's Demon: Gene Justice and the Complexity of Life*, 2000
Ridley, Matt, *The Red Queen: Sex and the Evolution of Human Nature*, 1993
Ridley, Matt, *Genome: The Autobiography of a Species in 23 Chapters*, 1999
Ridley, Matt, *The Agile Gene: How Nature Turns on Nurture*, 2003
Ridley, Matt, *Francis Crick: Discoverer of the Genetic Code*, 2006
Ruse, Michael, *Monad to Man: The Concept of Progress in Evolutionary Biology*, 1996
Ruse, Michael, *Can a Darwinian be a Christian?: The Relationship Between Science and Religion*, 2001
Ruse, Michael, *Darwin and Design: Does evolution have a purpose?*, 2003
Ruse, Michael, *The Evolution-Creation Struggle*, 2005
Ruse, Michael, *Darwinism and its Discontents*, 2006
Ruse, Michael, *Charles Darwin*, 2008
Russell, Robert John (ed.), *Evolutionary and Molecular Biology: Scientific Perspectives on Divine Action*, 1998
Sagan, Carl, *Cosmos*, 1980
Schaeffer, Francis A., *Genesis in Space and Time*, 1972
Schrodinger, Erwin, *What is Life?*, 1944
Scott, Eugenie, *Evolution vs. Creationism: An Introduction*, 2005
Sewell, Granville, *In the Beginning: and Other Essays on Intelligent Design*, 2010
Shapiro, Robert, *The Human Blueprint: The Race to Unlock the Secrets of Our Genetic Script*, 1991

Shermer, Michael, *Why Darwin Matters: The Case Against Intelligent Design*, 2006
Shuban, Neil, *Your Inner Fish: A Journey into the 3.5-Billion-Year History of the Human Body*, 2008
Silver, Lee M., *Remaking Eden: How Genetic Engineering and Cloning will Transform the American Family*, 1997
Silver, Lee M., *Challenging Nature: The Clash of Science and Spirituality at the New Frontiers of Life*, 2006
Simpson, George Gaylord, *This View of Life: The World of an Evolutionist*, 1947
Singh, Simon, *Big Bang: The Origin of the Universe*, 2004
Smolin, Lee, *The Life of the Cosmos*, 1997
Smolin, Lee, *The Trouble with Physics: The Rise of String Theory, the Fall of a Science, and What Comes Next*, 2006
Strobel, Lee, *The Case for a Creator*, 2004
Susskind, Leonard, *The Cosmic Landscape: String Theory and the Illusion of Intelligent Design*, 2006
Sykes, Bryan, *The Seven Daughters of Eve: The Science that Reveals our Genetic Ancestry*, 2001
Tattersall, Ian, *Becoming Human: Evolution and Human Uniqueness*, 1998
Tyson, Neil DeGrasse and Goldsmith, Donald, *Origins: Fourteen Billion Years of Cosmic Evolution*, 2004
Van Till, Howard J., 1989, *The Fourth Day: What the Bible and the Heavens are telling us about Creation*
Venter, J. Craig, *A Life Decoded: My Genome: My Life*, 2007
Walton, John, *The Lost World of Genesis One: Ancient Cosmology and the Origins* Debate, 2009
Ward, Keith, *God, Chance and Necessity*, 1996
Ward, Peter, and Brownlee, Donald, *The Life and Death of Planet Earth: How the New Science of Astrobiology Charts the Ultimate Fate of Our World*, 2002
Ward, Peter, and Brownlee, Donald, *Rare Earth: Why Complex Life is Uncommon in the Universe*, 2004
Watson, James, *The Double Helix*, 1980
Weinberg, Steven, *The First Three Minutes: A Modern View of the Origin of the Universe*, 1993
Weinberg, Steven, *Dreams of a Final Theory : The Scientist's Search for the Ultimate Laws of Nature*, 1992
Weiner, Jonathan, *The Beak of the Finch*, 1995
Wells, Johnathan, *Icons of Evolution: Science or Myth?: Why much of what we teach about evolution is wrong*, 2000

Whitehead, Alfred North, 1925, *Science and the Modern World*
Wilcox, David L., *God and Evolution: A Faith-Based Understanding*, 2004
Wilson, David Sloan, *Evolution for Everyone: How Darwin's Theory Can Change the Way We Think About Our Lives*, 2007
Wilson, E. O., *The Diversity of Life*, 1993
Wilson, E. O., *Consilience: The Unity of Knowledge*, 1998
Wilson, E. O., *The Creation: An Appeal to Save Life on Earth*, 2006
Wilson, John, *Uncommon Dissent: Intellectuals Who Find Darwinism Unconvincing*, 2004
Witham, Larry, *By Design: Science and the Search for God*, 2003
Witham, Larry, *Where Darwin Meets the Bible: Creationists and Evolutionists in America*, 2002
Woodward, Thomas, *Doubts about Darwin: A History of Intelligent Design*, 2003
Woodward, Thomas, *Darwin Strikes Back: Defending the Science of Intelligent Design*, 2006
Young, Davis & Stearley, Ralph, 2008, *The Bible, Rocks and Time: Geological Evidence for the Age of the Earth*
Zimmer, Carl, *Evolution: The Triumph of an Idea*, 2006

Glossary

amino acid

Critical to life as the building blocks of proteins.

Anthropic Principle

The concept that the laws of nature are compatible with the life observed in it and lead inevitably to the evolution of the universe and life, including humans in particular.

apoptosis

The normal programmed cell death that occurs in multicellular organisms.

Archaea

A group of single-celled organisms with no cell nucleus, yet unique from bacteria in that they contains genes more closely related to eukaryotes.

atavistic

Tendency to revert to ancestral types, like hind legs on whales.

bilateral symmetry

Organisms divided into roughly mirror image halves.

biomass

Biological material derived from living or recently living organisms.

bipedalism

Means of locomotion based on use of two feet and legs.

catastrophists

The idea that earth has been subject to sudden, violent, possibly worldwide catastrophic events.

category mistake

A property incorrectly assigned to an entity, assigning an entity to a class to which it does not belong.

chloroplasts

Organelles found in plant cells that conduct photosynthesis.

clade

A group in the tree of life consisting of a single ancestor and all of its descendents.

coccyx

The tailbone, the final segment in the vertebral column.

codons

The triplet sequence of nucleotide base pairs that defines the genetic DNA code.

colinearity

In genetics, the particular sequence of genes on a single chromosome.

differential reproduction

Heritable traits that give individuals a reproductive advantage in the next generation.

double helix

In molecular biology, the structure that contains the cell's DNA.

dysteleology

The philosophical view that existence has no ultimate cause from purposeful design.

Ediacarian

The geological period immediately preceding the Cambrian period.

endosymbiotic theory

The theory that mitochondria and chloroplasts originated as prokaryotic cells that were taken inside the eukaryotic cells.

epistemology

The nature of knowledge and the study of how we know what we know.

ethology

The study of animal behaviour.

eukaryote

An organism whose cells contain complex structures inside membranes, most notably the cell nucleus with genetic material.

exon

The sequence of a gene that directly codes for amino acids, as opposed to an intron.

genotype

The genes within an organism.

heliocentric

The theory that the solar system is centered on the sun.

homeotic genes

Genes that determine the body plan of an organism.

hominoid

The family of primates, including apes and humans.

homologous, homology

In biology, any similarities in organisms owing to shared ancestry.

homoplasy

Convergent evolution, the acquisition of the same biological trait in unrelated lineages.

HOX genes

DNA sequence in genes that regulate patterns of development in organisms.

intron

The DNA region within a gene that is not translated into protein, as opposed to exon.

lanugo

Fine, downy hair that grows on fetuses as a normal part of gestation, usually shed before birth.

laryngeal nerve

Nerve originating in the brain that innervates the muscles in the larynx.

microbial mats

Multi-layered sheets of micro-organisms that grow on the surfaces of different materials.

mitochondria

Membrane-enclosed organelle found in eukaryotic cells that generates most of the cell's supply of energy.

morphology

The study of the form and structure of an organism.

Neanderthal

An extinct member of the Homo genus with fossils first found in Europe.

nucleosynthesis

The process of creating new atomic nuclei from pre-existing nucleons.

nuclide

An atomic element identified by its nucleus constituents and energy state.

olfactory receptor

Neurons in cell membranes responsible for chemical detection of odors.

ontogeny

Describing the origin and development of an organism.

organelles

A specialized entity within a cell such as mitochondria that has a specific function.

paleontology

The study of prehistoric life, its evolution, and interaction with its environment, including the study of the fossil record.

phenotype

Any observable trait of an organism resulting from the expression of its genes, including its behaviour.

phyla

A biological taxon between Kingdom and Class, usually distinguished by a common body plan.

phylogenetic

The study of the evolutionary relatedness amoung various groups of organisms discovered through genetic sequencing data.

physiology

The study of the ways in which the bodies of living organisms work.

prokaryote

A group of single celled organisms that lack a cell nucleus.

pseudogene

Disabled relatives of functional genes that no longer have the ability to produce protein.

quarks

An theoretical elementary physical constituent of matter, combining to form protons and neutrons.

red shift

The increase in 'redness' frequency of light when the light source is moving away from the measuring location.

reductionist

An approach to understanding in which the nature of a complex entity can be completely understood by reducing the entity to the interaction and composition of its parts.

singularity

A point in time and space where forces cause matter to have an infinite density and zero volume.

splicing

In genetics, the modification of ribonucleic acids.

stasis

A period of little or no evolutionary change in a species.

stromatolites

Layered rocky structures in shallow water formed by the accretionary sedimentation of microorganisms.

supernova

A stellar explosion of extreme energy.

teleological

A view of nature that posits nature as having a property of design and purpose.

tetrapod

Vertebrate animals having four legs.

theropod

A group of dinosaurs linked to birds.

triplet code (see codons)

uniformitarian

The assumption that natural forces of cause and effect have operated from the start of the universe until now and apply everywhere.

varve lake

A lake characterized by an annual accumulated layer of sedimentary rock.

vertebrates

Chordate organisms with a backbone or spinal column.

vestigial

Homologous traits of organisms that seem to have lost most of their original function.

Index

Ahmanson, Howard Fieldstead 76, 77, 83
Alexander, Denis 14, 18, 22-25, 52-55, 185
Alpher, Ralph 33
amino acid ..146, 174, 175, 185
analogous............167, 170, 200
anthropic.................36-38, 220
aortic arch 189
apoptosis............................173
Archaea...............................191
Archaeopteryx 151, 152, 155
atavistic...............................188
Augustine.............................57
Bacon, Francis 14, 58
Barr, Steven 114, 115, 220
Behe, Michael....82, 83, 89, 90, 99, 100, 114, 120, 122, 129, 183, 184, 197, 212, 220
Berlinski, David...............20, 28
bilateral symmetry 167
biogeography 155, 156, 160, 198, 205
bipedalism 154
Bohr, Niels............................71
Bradley, Walter L. 80, 81
bristlecone pine.....................43
Bryan, William Jennings 63, 227
Cambrian ...40, 45, 53, 87, 150, 171, 208
Carroll, Sean.......170, 171, 184, 194, 195, 206-208, 220
catastrophists 144
category mistake.............22, 23
Chapman, Bruce 83
Chesterton, G.K. 18, 71
chloroplasts..........................45
chromosome 167, 177-179, 208
clade..................................196
coccyx................................188
colinearity 178
Collins, Francis..... 50, 51, 116-118, 177, 178, 211, 221
common descent....13, 52, 112, 143-150, 158, 177-190, 197-199, 202, 205-214, 218
common design....13, 144-148, 182, 187, 190, 197, 198, 202, 207-212
continental drift 160, 162
convergence........159, 198, 199
Copernicus........27, 52, 70, 110
Coyne, Jerry...... 151-154, 162, 166, 171- 173, 180, 188, 210, 211, 221
Crick, Francis 49, 65, 146, 221, 226
Cuvier, Georges.....................59
cytochrome c 192
Darrow, Charles....................63
Darwin, Charles. 17, 47-49, 59-61, 75, 81-87, 90, 93, 94, 97-99, 105, 106, 114, 115, 12-125, 132, 133, 143-157, 163-166, 170, 180, 183, 184, 187, 200, 202, 207, 212, 215, 220-228
Davis, Percival......................82
Dawkins, Richard 38, 81, 82, 114, 117, 215, 221, 224
Dembski, William.... 82-84, 87, 91, 99, 104, 122, 123, 133, 221
Denton, Michael 80, 81, 221
Descartes, Rene 58
differential reproduction....168, 185

dinosaur... 47, 53, 66, 151, 152, 180
Dobzhansky, Theodosius.... 55, 134, 135, 222
double helix.................. 49, 146
Drosophila.................. 167, 168
dysteleological 126
Eddington, Arthur 29
Ediacarian 171
Eichhorn, Johann 61
Einstein, Albert .. 28-31, 34, 39, 70, 71, 90, 225
Eldredge, Niles................... 150
embryology 165, 166, 171, 173, 184, 198, 208
endosymbiotic theory.......... 193
Eohippus 152
epistemology........................ 14
ethologist.............................. 81
eukaryote.............. 45, 192, 193
exon...................................... 182
Falk, Darrel 55, 222
Ferris, Timothy 28, 31, 222
Fowler, Thomas . 144, 175-178, 217, 222
fruit fly 49, 167
Galileo.................. 17, 27, 121
Gamow, George 32, 33, 93
genome. 50, 168, 176-181, 185, 202, 208-211
geology 17, 63, 194
Gerhart, John..... 169, 200, 201, 223
Giberson, Karl... 105, 106, 121, 122, 132, 133, 139, 180, 222
Gingerich, Owen 109-112, 170, 216-218, 222
GLO 180
Gonzalez, Guillermo...... 77, 78
Gould, Stephen Jay 45, 150, 189, 222
Gray, Asa 61, 192, 208

Gray, Terry................ 192, 207
Haarsma, Loren. 107, 108, 131, 132, 141, 142, 158, 159, 206, 223
Haeckel, Ernst............. 85, 165
Haldane, J.B.S.................. 150
Haught, John 109, 113, 123, 124, 130, 134, 223
heliocentric.................... 28, 70
hemoglobin 192, 213
Herman, Robert.................... 33
hippopotamus..................... 153
homeotic genes................... 167
hominoid 154
homologous................ 199, 200
homology .. 148, 168, 199, 201, 207
homoplasy 195
HOX genes. 167, 168, 178, 207
Hoyle, Fred 31-34, 75, 129, 223
Hubble, Edwin 29
Hume, David........................ 59
Huxley, Thomas........... 61, 152
hypothesis 15, 38, 39, 112, 160, 161, 173, 198, 203
Ichneumonidae................... 133
intron.......................... 181, 182
irreducibly complex 87, 114, 124, 183
Jastrow, Robert 29, 34, 223
Johnson, Phillip..... 78, 82, 106, 114, 122-129, 221, 223
Kaufmann, Stuart................. 44
Kenyon, Dean 81, 82
Kepler............................. 28, 70
Kirschner, Marc 169, 200, 201, 208, 223
Klassen, Glen R. 119, 124, 140
Krischner, Marc 169
Lamaitre, Georges................ 32
Lamarck, Jean 59

Lamoureux, Denis 103, 106, 114, 124-129, 184, 185, 223, 224
lanugo 166
laryngeal nerve 189
Lennox, John 22, 23
Lewis, C.S. 56, 224
Lewontin 125
Lewontin, Richard 20
Luskin, Casey 190-197
Lyell, Charles 59, 145
Lystrosaurus 161
MacDowell, Josh 87
MacDowell, Sean 87, 91
macroevolution 76, 143, 206, 207
malaria 164, 213
Margulis, Lynn 193, 194
marsupial 158-161
materialism 67, 83, 125, 126, 136
McGrath, Alister .. 51, 103, 117, 224
Mendel, Gregor ... 49, 146, 168, 183, 225
metaphysical 21, 24, 36, 87, 96, 103, 123, 126, 127, 139, 149
methodological naturalism ... 22
Meyer, Stephen 24, 82, 83
microbial mats 44
microevolution.... 143, 206, 207
Miller, Keith 106, 126, 127, 192, 208
Miller, Kenneth . 115, 120, 125, 135, 152, 154, 171, 184, 202-207, 215, 216
Miller-Urey 85
Mills, David 94, 99, 224
mitochondria 45
Monod, Jacques 11, 12
Moore, Aubrey 124

Moreland, J.P. 129, 130, 224
Morgan, Thomas Hunt .. 49, 146
morphology .. 17, 145, 148, 166, 198-200
Morris, Henry . 66, 77, 104, 126
Morris, Simon Conway 159
Murphy, Nancy 78
naturalism 13, 18, 21, 24, 25, 82-84, 87, 103, 113, 126, 127, 139, 149
Neanderthal 155
Nelson, Paul 83
Newman, John Henry 140
Newton, Isaac 27, 28, 58, 90, 121, 122, 220
Noll, Mark 67-69, 225
nucleosynthesis 75
nuclide 42, 43
octopus 188, 199, 200
olfactory receptor 181, 211
Olsen, Roger L 80, 81
ontogeny 165
organelles 45, 193
Origen 57
paleontology ... 17, 49, 198, 202
Paley, William 48, 59, 114
Pangea 160
Pascal, Blaise 37
Penzias, Arno 31, 33, 35, 39
Perakh, Mark 99, 225
Peters, Ted 103, 104, 225
phenotype 170
phyla 45, 46, 53, 144, 208
phylogenetic 191, 193, 196, 199
phylogeny 165
physiology 17, 194, 200
placental 158, 159
Plantinga, Alvin 94, 95, 225
plate tectonics 160
Polkinghorne, John 56, 103, 225

Pope, Alexander 27
Price, George McCready 63, 64, 66
prokaryote 45, 191
pseudogene 180, 181, 209
pseudogenes 179-182, 187, 209, 210
quarks 27, 32
Ramm, Bernard 64
red shift 34, 40
reductionist 19
relativity 15, 28, 29, 39, 70, 71, 90
retina 188
Richards, Jay 77, 222
Ridley, Mark 168, 182, 183, 225, 226
Rimmer, Harry 64
ring species 157
Rokas, Antonis 194, 195
Ruse, Michael ... 75, 82, 95, 96, 100, 102, 140, 145, 152, 157, 162, 163, 207, 226
Rushdoony, Rousas 77
Russell, Bertrand 19
Sagan, Carl 19
salamanders 157
Sandage, Allan 35
science 13
scientism 18, 19, 130
Scofield, C.I. 58
Scopes, John T. 63, 75, 224
Scott, Eugenie 216, 217
sexual recombination 185
Shermer, Michael.. 97- 99, 139, 226
Shubin, Neil 153
sickle cell anemia 164
singularity 30-32
Smoot, George 35
specified complexity 84, 123
splicing 181

Sputnik 65
stasis 149
Stein, Ben 77
Stenger, Victor 97
Strobel, Lee 24
stromatolites 44
supernova 51
Susskind, Leonard 36, 227
teleological 111, 125, 140
Temple, Frederick 215
Tennyson, Alfred Lord. 48, 133
tetrapod 153
Thaxton, Charles B. 80, 81
theropod 151, 152
Tiktaalik 153, 155
triplex code 146, 168, 174
uniformitarian 145
Ussher, James 57, 58, 62
Van Till, Howard J 113
varve lake 43
vertebrates . 148, 153, 166, 172, 201
vestigial 153, 187, 188
vitamin C 180, 209, 210, 213
von Bauer, Karl Ernst 165
Wallace, Alfred Russel . 47, 75, 145, 156
warbler 157
Warfield, B.B. 67
Watson, James ... 49, 50, 51, 65, 146
Weinberg, Steven 71, 227
Wells, Jonathan 83, 84, 192, 227
whale 148, 152, 155
Whitcomb, J.C. 66, 225
White, Ellen 63
Wilberforce, Samuel 61
Wilcox, David L. 135-138, 227
Wilson, Robert .. 29, 31, 33, 35, 39, 227, 228
Woese, Carl 190, 191, 192

Woodward, Thomas 93, 94, 228

Zimmer, Carl 135, 141, 228

A Reasonable God

www.ingramcontent.com/pod-product-compliance
Lightning Source LLC
Chambersburg PA
CBHW020354170426
43200CB00005B/161